CW01483763

ILLUSTRATORS
ANNUAL **2017**

Jury 2017

HARRIET BIRKINSHAW
STEVEN GUARNACCIA
JEAN-FRANÇOIS MARTIN
ARIANNA SQUILLONI
DANIELA STAMATIADI

An event by:

President
FRANCO BONI

General Manager
ANTONIO BRUZZONE

Commercial Director Italy
MARCO MOMOLI

Exhibition Manager
ELENA PASOLI

**Bologna Children's Book Fair
Show Office**
MARZIA SAMPAOLI
CRISTINA PANCALDI

Illustrators Exhibition
DEANNA BELLUTI
MARIA IRENE VENTURI

**Bologna Children's Book Fair
Piazza Costituzione, 6
40128 Bologna, Italy
www.bolognachildrensbookfair.com
bookfair@bolognafiere.it
illustratori@bolognafiere.it**

ILLUSTRATORS
ANNUAL 2017

CONTENTS

What is the most precious lesson you have learnt from your long career as an illustrator of children's books?

To look beyond your own nose, to stay curious while keeping faith with yourself.

ROTRAUT
SUSANNE
BERNER

**COVER ARTIST
OF THE ILLUSTRATORS
ANNUAL 2017**

Besides having made your own books as an author and illustrator, you have also illustrated books written by others (including works by great writers like Hans Magnus Enzensberger and Sylvia Plath). What is the difference between the two types of work?

It is easier for me to illustrate writings by other authors: a natural distance that permits a different kind of gaze is created. For me distance is an important premise. I need it to be able to approach a story, its language, its specific character in a way that is always new, from different perspectives. With my stories I have to create this distance artificially, which is not always easy.

In the *laudatio* in your honor at the time of the assignment of the Hans Christian Andersen Award, the chairperson of the jury, Patsy Aldana, spoke of the courage with which you have also come to terms with "dark themes" in your books, and the way you have treated them "without taboos, but at the same time with caution." What is the right way to approach difficult themes in picture books for children?

Since I was a timid little girl myself, I am conscious of the therapeutic power of art: precisely through the representation of scenes of cruelty, violence and death, as one often encounters in fables, I could look my fears in the face and exorcise them in that way. Of course my reasoning faculty is always very active when I work, but the creative impulses, the why and how to translate certain themes into images and words, come from different, multiple sources. To follow primary impulses is therefore much more interesting than paying attention to pedagogical, moral or correct "concerns" that of course arise in me as well, which I have to combat. The way I come to terms with death, illness, fears or violence in my books is therefore something that pertains not so much to a decision-making process as to my way of being as a person.

Reason tells me, however, that at all ages people have to come to grips with themes of all kinds, and we can expect everyone to find a way to cope with them. I cannot really care for my young readers, because I don't actually know them. Instead, I cherish the hope and faith that literature and art can reach those who are touched by the stories I tell in the right moment.

Following a consolidated tradition, the Hans Christian Andersen Award winner is invited to draw the *Illustrators Annual*'s cover; this year Rotraut Susanne Berner is the creator of the illustration that will be featured in her exhibition entitled "IllustrEATing."

Rotraut Susanne Berner grew up in the countryside in the 1950s in Germany. She studied graphic design in Munich and started her working life designing book-jackets for adult books, with a focus on illustration.

For many years she has been designing and illustrating books for adults and now mainly for children. She also writes her own stories. She was influenced by the German illustrators Walter Trier and Wilhelm Busch. She is probably best known for her so-called "Wimmelbuch," picture-stories without words, like the *Number-Devil* with Hans Magnus Enzensberger—her books for toddlers which have been translated into many languages.

Rotraut Susanne Berner has received many artistic awards such as the Deutscher Jugendliteraturpreis for illustration in 2006 for her lifetime achievement and the Hans Christian Andersen award in 2016. She lives in Munich, where she also edits illustrated booklets, called *Die Tollen Hefte*, a series founded by her husband Armin Abmeier. As a founder and curator of the German Foundation of Illustration, she is engaged in all areas of this art form to promote its role and relevance in society.

FROM "EINFACH ALLES. DIE WORTSCHATZKISTE." KLETT KINDERBUCHVERLAG. 2009

FROM "NACHT-WIMMELBUCH." GERSTENBERG VERLAG. 2008

What is necessary to make a great "Wimmelbuch"?

The desire to tell a story: precisely because the books have no text, the focus is entirely on the narrative power of images. This is a big challenge and also a remarkable limitation, from the viewpoint of both form and content. But like any "handicap" this too produces a particular "artistic form." To narrate a story in episodes with many characters without words, that takes place in a precise time span, calls for great clarity, for example. People can be made recognizable by means of their physical appearance, but also through specific character traits. To this end, one can use different stylistic tools and emphasize, for example, clothing, gestures or specific habits. These books, like any literary text, also call for small or great "dramas" that have to be made interesting for very young readers. It is great when the readers have the sensation that something new is always there to be discovered, and therefore in the narration of my books there are different levels of observation, with different degrees of difficulty. There is a level of observation, for example, also for the youngest readers who can only look, find and point. To explore the world and to give a name to things and people.

Nowadays is it harder to capture the attention of a child with a traditional means like a picture book than it was thirty or forty years ago?

Probably. When I was a child images were not such a preponderant presence in public space, so in general one undoubtedly paid closer attention to them. However, the way children react to a traditional illustrated book today is a question that depends on whether and how they have learned to come to terms with the various media. Personally, I believe that picture books are a perfect medium for very young children. They can observe the images in an absolutely independent way, at their own pace, whenever they want to. And the book, which is a personal, clearly visible object, to which to become attached, always available, is something completely different from a technological device. Tablets or computers offer specific and extraordinary opportunities, but for me it is important that little children learn to explore true reality before they explore virtual reality.

You have worked in the world of picture books for many years. What are the biggest changes you have witnessed over the course of your career?

There have always been beautiful and ugly, ambitious and insignificant illustrated books; in this sense, very little has changed over the last four decades. The big change is the ever-growing number of illustrated books and the resulting difficulty of getting your bearings in the midst of this mass of publications. The relationship with the images that increasingly dominate public space has become more important. Learning to read images, to understand context and subtext, to find the aesthetic criteria and to approach art in a natural way: all this constitutes a discipline in itself, which even though it is taught is in any case widely neglected in schools and universities. And this has repercussions also for the reception of those media that rely more on text content than visual content, and do not pay sufficient attention to the aspects of applied art.

FROM "LÜGEN HABEN KURZE OHREN." BY RAINER ERLINGER. OMNIBUS. COVER ILLUSTRATION. 2007

How important is it for an illustrator of children's books to know how to see the world through the eyes of a child?

Perhaps the secret of the classics for children is that their authors are able to observe the world from both an adult's perspective and that of a child. I would like to respond with a quotation from Erich Kästner:

Look, most people take off their childhood the way they would take off an old hat. They forget it, just as they would forget a phone number that is no longer valid. The life they have lived seems like a seasoned sausage, consumed a bit at a time, and what has been eaten no longer exists [. . .]. Now most people live like that [. . .]. First they were children, then they became adults, but now what are they? Only he who becomes an adult and remains a child is a man.

FROM BOLOGNA TO THE WORLD AND BACK

Over fifty years have passed since 1967, when in Bologna, "la dotta," home of the first university in the western world, the Illustrators Exhibition was born. Three years earlier, in 1964, there had been the first edition of what was originally known as the International Fair for Children's and Young Adult Literature, a space that in those crucial years of a true revolution in children's publishing immediately attracted publishers, illustrators, authors and other sector professionals who wanted to meet and to share ideas, perspectives and projects. The Fair rapidly became a place of reference for this very lively sector. The organizers soon understood the importance of what had been set in motion in Bologna, and decided to accompany each edition of the Fair with an Illustrators Exhibition.

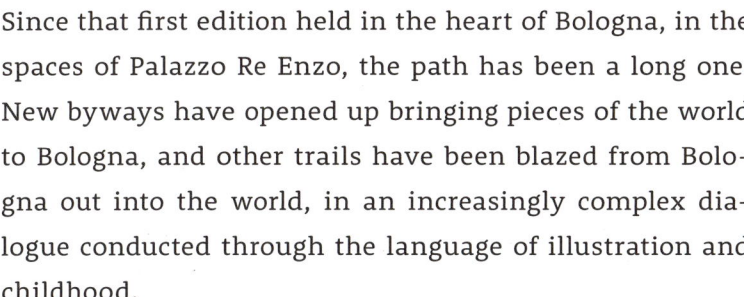

ROTRAUT SUSANNE BERNER FROM "DAS KIND UND DIE KATZE [DIE TOLLEN HEFTE]." BY INGRID BACHÉR. BÜCHERGILDE. 2010

Since that first edition held in the heart of Bologna, in the spaces of Palazzo Re Enzo, the path has been a long one. New byways have opened up bringing pieces of the world to Bologna, and other trails have been blazed from Bologna out into the world, in an increasingly complex dialogue conducted through the language of illustration and childhood.

Right from the first iterations, the exhibition has attracted illustrators from all countries, but it is necessary to mention two "vectors" that have contributed to reinforce its global character. On the one hand, the international juries, which on a regular basis, since 1976, have involved leading professionals from the world of children's publishing, internationally acclaimed illustrators, editors and critics from different geographical areas. Personalities that have brought their own artistic, cultural and cognitive backgrounds to Bologna, to approach a difficult task (just remember that at the last edition there were over 3,000 participating illustrators, for a total of nearly 16,000 works!).

Many of them, after returning home, have become true ambassadors of the exhibition, and their efforts have been very useful over the years to bring new waves of artists to Bologna from their countries, constantly expanding the initiative's horizons.

TAIWAN. 2016

A second vector of internationalization has been the *Illustrators Annual*, the book you are presently holding in your hands. Though a book was printed from the very first editions on, it was only in 1976 that it became a full-color publication: the Annual thus gathered together, for the first time, the works of the selected artists, helping them to be discovered also by those who did not have the possibility of physically attending the fair. This somehow closed a circle: the illustrations originally invented for books were gathered for the first time in a volume designed to focus on illustration.

TOKYO. 2016

So it should come as no surprise that just two years after the organization of the first international jury and the publication of the first true Annual, the exhibition made a great leap forward, a literally intercontinental leap. In 1978 the exhibition arrived for the first time in Japan, thanks to the collaboration with the Itabashi Art Museum of Tokyo, which since then has hosted the show every year, making it circulate in various other museums in that country. In recent years this international circulation has also expanded to new areas like China and the United States, countries that not only host the exhibition but also publish foreign editions of the Annual.

TOKYO. 2016

BEIJING. 2016

Over the years the exhibition, as an internationally acknowledged case of Italian excellence, has also assumed the role of an ambassador of Italian culture, as is borne out by initiatives like the regular presence at BookExpo America of the Italian illustrators selected in the latest edition, the exhibition "Illustrazione per ragazzi: Eccellenze italiane" that is still touring the world, thanks to the collaboration between the Bologna Children's Book Fair and the Italian Cultural Institutes of Madrid, Berlin, Sofia, Shanghai and Cairo, or the presence of a delegation of Italian illustrators in Iran during the Tehran International Book Fair, where Italy is the guest nation in May 2017. Likewise, we should not overlook the exhibition "Artists and Masterpieces of Illustration. 50 Illustrators Exhibitions 1967–2016," to mark the 50th anniversary, which after its debut in Bologna has also been seen in Wrocław (Poland) and Milan.

TAIWAN. 2016

ROTRAUT SUSANNE BERNER. EDITORIAL FOR "DIE WELT"

NARRATING THE SCOPE OF THE FAIR THROUGH ILLUSTRATION

For some years now, in keeping with the evolution of the publishing houses themselves, Bologna Children's Book Fair has expanded its perspective to include the world of digital publishing, apps, animation and licensing. Many different spirits and approaches, but all sharing the common denominator of content for young people. A fair that goes beyond copyright exchange and increasingly takes on the character of a creative workshop, a cradle of innovation.

To sum all this up in one image, Bologna Children's Book Fair has turned to the heart of creativity, represented in an outstanding way by the protagonists of the Illustrators Exhibition, to rethink its own visual identity. For the first time in its history, BCBF has decided to narrate its true scope, relying on the talent of an illustrator, Daniele Castellano, one of those selected in the 2016 edition of the exhibition, who has worked for months with the guidance of the graphic design studio Chialab, to create the Chimera, in all its versions, which now represents the 2017 edition of the event in the world. A very positive experiment that will become stable over time, involving a new artist each year, chosen from those discovered by the Illustrators Exhibition.

BOLOGNA
DIGITAL
MEDIA

AWARDS

BOLOGNA
ILLUSTRATORS
EXHIBITION

ILLUSTRATORS
SURVIVAL
CORNER

TRANSLATORS
CENTRE

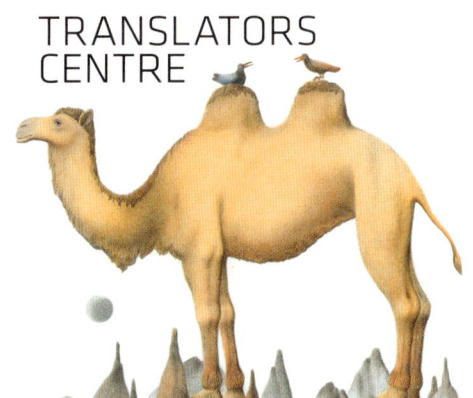

ROTRAUT SUSANNE BERNER. "NACHT-WIMMELBUCH.". GERSTENBERG VERLAG. 2008

THE ILLUSTRATORS EXHIBITION DOES NOT
END IN BOLOGNA: AFTER THE FAIR,
IT GOES ON A LONG TOUR OF MORE
THAN TWO YEARS IN SEVERAL COUNTRIES
AND CULTURES.

THANKS TO THE COLLABORATION BETWEEN
THE BOLOGNA CHILDREN'S BOOK FAIR AND
THE ITABASHI ART MUSEUM – TOKYO FOR
OVER THIRTY YEARS, THE ILLUSTRATORS
EXHIBITION IS A GO-TO EVENT, EAGERLY
AWAITED EACH YEAR BY INDUSTRY ~
PROFESSIONALS, SCHOOLS AND FAMILIES:
SEVERAL MUSEUMS OPEN THEIR DOORS
TO WELCOME THIS GREAT ILLUSTRATION
FESTIVAL FROM THE WORLD OVER,
ORGANIZING PROFESSIONAL MEETINGS
AND WORKSHOPS FOR CHILDREN.

TOKYO, 2016

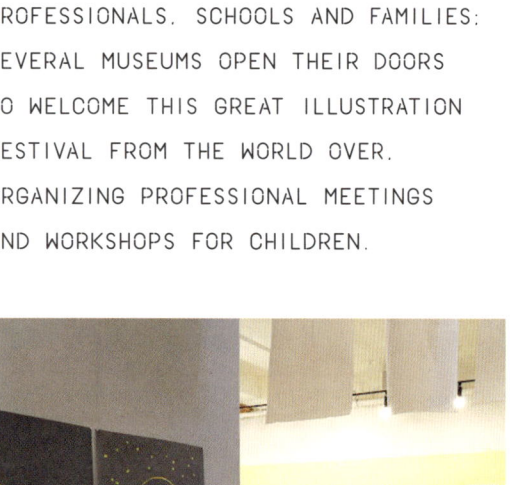

CHICAGO, 2016

BEIJING, 2016

THE 2017 ILLUSTRATORS EXHIBITION'S
TOUR IN JAPAN:

ITABASHI ART MUSEUM
(TOKYO)
1 JULY – 13 AUGUST 2017

OTANI MEMORIAL ART MUSEUM
(NISHINOMIYA)
19 AUGUST – 24 SEPTEMBER 2017

KAWARA ART MUSEUM
(TAKAHAMA)
30 SEPTEMBER – 29 OCTOBER 2017

ISHIKAWA NANAO ART MUSEUM
(NANAO)
3 NOVEMBER – 10 DECEMBER 2017

STARTING IN MAY 2016 WITH THE INAUGURATION AT BEIJING'S NATIONAL LIBRARY. THE TOUR IN CHINA THIS YEAR INCLUDES ONCE MORE SIX CITIES WHERE THE EXHIBITION IS SHOWN AT MAJOR MUSEUMS AND LIBRARIES.

TAIWAN. 2016

ROTRAUT SUSANNE BERNER. "AMBROSE BIERCE TOLLES HEFT." FROM "DIE TOLLEN HEFTE 36." 2011

BEIJING. 2016

AND THAT'S NOT ALL! TAIPEI: AFTER BEING SHOWN AT THE CHIANG KAI-SHEK MEMORIAL HALL. THE EXHIBITION NOW GOES TO THE HUASHAN CREATIVITY PARK. A LIVELY DISTRICT ENTIRELY DEDICATED TO ART. AND THEN CHICAGO. WHERE THE COLUMBIA COLLEGE MAKES THE EXHIBITION A SUBJECT OF STUDY WITH ACCOMPANYING WORKSHOPS. OTHER VENUES ARE ALSO IN THE PIPELINE AND. AFTER THE FAIR. THE EXHIBITION WILL BE HOSTED IN BOLOGNA'S CIVIC ARCHEOLOGICAL MUSEUM. ONE OF THE MOST PRESTIGIOUS CULTURAL LOCATIONS OF THE CITY.

19

ILLUSTRATORS EXHIBITION
JURY REPORT

We arrived in Bologna from Barcelona, Paris, Athens, London and New York, two editors and three illustrators, each with a personal set of criteria of tastes and prejudices for one kind of illustration or another. By the time we left Bologna, many of these tastes and prejudices had been turned upside-down and questioned, tested and finally set aside in favor of looking with fresh eyes at the 16,000 works that greeted us when we arrived.

From the two black Mercedes waiting to take us to and from our HQ at Hotel Roma every morning and evening, to the fact that we five occupied the 3rd floor of the otherwise empty hotel, we felt like a crack team of illustration professionals flown into Bologna on a special mission: to choose the best entries from a pool of more than 3,000 artists, each submitting 5 images.

Bologna during the Children's Book Fair is a city overrun with illustrators, editors, agents and publishers. Hotels are fully booked, sometimes years in advance, and getting into a restaurant can be as hard as getting an invite to a Hollywood premiere. The fairgrounds themselves are swarming with workers in the children's book trade, loosening ties in the heat, donning scarves in the cold, talking, toasting, trading.

But now our cars dropped us in an unfamiliar corner of the fair, at a pavilion that is empty at this time of year. Out tumbled this groggy (but still razor sharp) SWAT team of jurors. We walked up the eerily motionless escalator and into a vast room dominated by what seemed like endless rows of industrial tables nearly buckling under the weight of some 16,000 illustrations. Their weight wasn't only due to the paper they were drawn, painted, collaged and printed on, but to the hopes of the artists and the solemn and sometimes intimidating responsibility we felt as jurors.

We were there to include, not exclude. We were looking for the best, yes, but also those illustrations that seemed most representative of the state of children's book illustration today.

Our expectations changed as the days progressed. As one juror said, "At first, I didn't think there was much strong work, that there were only a few really good pieces. But as we got rid of some pieces, we began to see more clearly through the works. The strongest pieces emerged slowly."

At first we were afraid that our different sensibilities might not be able to be reconciled, but we quickly found a group of images we all agreed on. Only towards the end did our most personal and deeply held tastes come forward. As one of the jurors said, "I was so surprised that I made so many choices no one else liked. The first day was the hardest, psychologically."

We let go of the idea of looking only for work appropriate for children, though we continued to test our selections

21

against their child-appropriateness. But we also felt that the purpose of the exhibition was to present the strongest narrative work from the submissions.

Three artists who were at first rejected outright were in the end almost unanimous choices. When we were forced to defend a piece to the other jurors, we sometimes found ourselves realizing that we were less committed to a selection than we thought. On the other hand, we selected things we might never have chosen alone, because the other jurors convinced us of the virtues of those pieces. Another juror said, "Of course, there were very nice pieces that we didn't choose."

We found that in some cases our national identities or the market we came from affected our judgment. And the illustrators and the editors often had differing perspectives. On the other hand, with so much work accessible to anyone anywhere with a computer, the cultural differences between illustrators seemed to melt in the heat of the Internet. We found among the entries a Japanese illustrator whose work was in the style of Indian folk painting, and a Middle Eastern-themed image that turned out to have been made by an Italian. And one Russian artist made a version of Red Riding Hood set in Southeast Asia.

The days were long. We had lunch and dinner together every day and that gave us a necessary break, reminding us that we were human beings with shared values, even if our tastes in illustration diverged. The meals, and the three days isolated in a distant pavilion of the fair, with no other social contact outside the group, allowed a certain level of trust to be developed.

Among the things we noticed in the illustrations submitted this year: lots of foxes and whales (has the fox's time come to be the antihero?); lots of very geometric architecture, and at the same time lots of lushly rendered jungle and forest; almost abstract images, as illustrators pared down their visual imagery to the minimum.

At the end, one of the jurors suggested we each choose one artist, as a "gift" to ourselves, without consulting the other jurors. It was in high spirits that we each struck out, like children on a treasure hunt, to look for those pieces that spoke perhaps only to ourselves.

HARRIET BIRKINSHAW grew up in England and attended the University of Warwick, where she studied English and American Literature. After graduating, she moved to London and started working in the picture book editorial department at children's publisher Andersen Press. While there, she worked with some of the best-known illustrators in the United Kingdom, including David McKee, Michael Foreman and Quentin Blake. In 2014, she moved from Andersen Press to Nobrow, an independent publisher of comics, graphic novels, and picture books under their children's imprint Flying Eye Books. In her role as Senior Commissioning Editor, she sources illustration talent from around the world across both book series and helps budding new artists to develop their work into publishable narratives.

STEVEN GUARNACCIA is an illustrator and designer, and Associate Professor of Illustration at Parsons The New School for Design, where he was the director of the Illustration Program from 2004 to 2011. He was previously the art director of the "Op-Ed" page of "The New York Times." During his thirty-five-year career as an internationally recognized illustrator he has worked for major magazines and newspapers, including "The New York Times," "Abitare," "Rolling Stone" and "Domus," created murals for Disney Cruise Line, and exhibition drawings for a show of Achille Castiglioni's work at the Museum of Modern Art. He is the author of books on popular culture and design, including *Black and White, a book on the absence of color*, published by Chronicle Books. Guarnaccia has designed watches and packaging for Swatch, and greeting cards for the Museum of Modern Art. He has won awards from AIGA, the Art Directors Club, and the Bologna Children's Book Fair, and has exhibited his work in one-man shows in the United States and Europe. His children's books include *Goldilocks and the Three Bears: A Tale Moderne*, *The Three Little Pigs: An Architectural Tale* and *Cinderella: A Fashionable Tale*, all published by Corraini Edizioni in Italy and Abrams in the United States.

JEAN-FRANÇOIS MARTIN was born in Paris in 1967 and studied at the Lycée du Livre et des Arts Graphiques and at the École Nationale Supérieure des Arts Appliqués et des Métiers d'Arts in Paris. Before becoming an illustrator, he started his career as an art director at Bayard Presse. He currently works for different publishers, including Thierry Magnier, Hélium, Albin Michel and Flammarion and for the press, both in France, for "Libération," "Télérama," "Le Monde," "XXI," and abroad, for "The New York Times," "The New Yorker," "The Guardian," "The Washington Post," "The Wall Street Journal," "Businessweek," "L'Actualité" and "The Progressive." Jean-François Martin is also a member of "2 œufs bacon p'tites patates," a group of graphic artists. In 2011 he won the BolognaRagazzi Award for Fiction, and in 2012 the Grand Prix de l'Illustration from the Musée de l'Illustration Jeunesse de Moulins for his work on Aesop's *Fables*. He has been awarded several prizes for his illustrations by AI-American Illustration. He is the author of a short animated film titled *L'inventeur*.

DANIELA STAMATIADI is a graduate of the Athens School of Fine Arts. She works in Athens, Greece, as a painter, illustrator and visual arts teacher in private colleges. She has been a freelance children's book illustrator since 2000, creating over a hundred books. In 2010 she received the Greek IBBY award and in 2012 the EBGE award for her illustrations. She was also invited to represent Greece at Salon Du Livre 2012, Paris. Daniela has taken part in numerous painting and illustration exhibitions both in Greece and abroad. Since 2010 she has cooperated with the Frissiras Gallery and the Frissiras Museum. In the year 2013 she received two EBGE prizes and was also assigned an Andersen Award nomination. In 2016 she won the Peter Pan Prize for best translated book from the Swedish IBBY for her book *Sabelle's Red Dress*. She also had a solo illustration exhibition with the title "En annan plats" ("Another Place") at Gotlands Konstmuseum in Sweden. She is represented by the Astound illustration agency.

ARIANNA SQUILLONI was born in Milan in 1976 where she studied Classical Literature and specialized in Linguistics and Philosophical Logic. She has lived in Barcelona since 2002, where she became interested in children's literature and in 2008 opened A buen paso, a publishing company for curious wanderers specialized in picture books and books with illustrations. She works with specialized magazines in Spain and other countries, including "Hors cadres[s]" and its Spanish version "Fuera de margen," takes part in workshops and debates, and offers lectures and classes in workshops and master's courses for writers, illustrators, librarians and teachers. She sometimes writes for children (*L'estate e tutto il resto*, Topipittori, 2016; *En casa de mis abuelos*, Ekaré, 2011, in Italy *A casa dei nonni*, Donzelli, 2012), as well as a general audience (*En el laberinto de la palabra, Guía de viaje*, Pantalia, 2014; *El verano de John Silver*, Editorial Milrazones, 2017). One of her passions is studying living and dead languages.

2017 BOLOGNA ILLUSTRATORS EXHIBITION

PUBLISHER'S NOTE:

AS STATED IN THE EXHIBITION REGULATIONS,
EACH ILLUSTRATOR SUBMITTED TO THE JURY
A SEQUENCE OF FIVE IMAGES, WHICH IDEALLY
FORM A STORY. IN SOME CASES, WE DECIDED
TO REPRODUCE ONLY SOME OF THE ILLUS-
TRATIONS SO AS TO HIGHLIGHT THE STRENGTHS
THAT THE JURY SAW IN THE WORK OF EACH
ARTIST. BUT WE ALSO DECIDED TO MAIN-
TAIN THE ORIGINAL NUMBERS IN THE CAPTIONS
OF THE ILLUSTRATIONS THAT WERE PRESENTED.
WHERE NOT EXPLICITLY STATED OTHERWISE,
ILLUSTRATORS HAVE NOT BEEN PREVIOUSLY
PUBLISHED ELSEWHERE.

"THE ORCHARD." LA JOIE DE LIRE. GENÈVE. 2017
"KAMASUTRA PARA DOMINGOS LLUVIOSOS." IMPEDIMENTA. MADRID. 2016
"UN REGALO PARA SILVIA." EDELVIVES. MADRID. 2015
"EL INVENTOR DE PÀJAROS." SM. MADRID. 2014

Mr. Méliès • Graphite, wax, mixed media • Fiction

Spain • *Alicante, 6 September 1983*

ximoabadia@gmail.com • 0034 622108949

XIMO ABADIA

XIMOABADIA.COM

1

3

ÉCOLE ÉMILE COHL
DIRECTOR: PHILIPPE RIVIÈRE
COORDINATOR: ISABELLE CHATELLARD

2

4

1 OLD WORLD MONKEYS: FACES   2 OLD WORLD MONKEYS: ATTITUDES   3 NEW WORLD MONKEYS: ATTITUDES   4 NEW WORLD MONKEYS: FACES

CLAIRE AGNELLI

Untitled • Gouache • Non fiction

France • *Puyricard, 31 December 1994*

claire.agnelli@etudiants.cohl.fr • 0033 622826256

4

2

3

2 EVERYTHING IS CHANGING   3 HE OPENS A TAILOR SHOP AT A THREE-WAY INTERSECTION AND SHARP DRESSERS APPEAR ON THE STREET
4 GRANDFATHER, FATHER AND SON MAKE SUITS IN THE SAME PLACE   5 EVERYTHING IS CHANGING AND MANY TAILOR SHOPS HAVE DISAPPEARED IN THE CITY

JAESUN AHN

Untitled · Ink and digital media · Fiction
Korea · *Daegu, 4 March 1976*
jaejaea@naver.com · 0082 1057127129

LYCÉE CORVISART, PARIS
DIRECTOR: MARIE-LAURE BERENGUIER
COORDINATOR: LAURENT CORVAISIER

5

CHLOÉ ALMÉRAS

La baigneuse (The Swimmer) • Gouache • Fiction

France • *Fontenay-aux-Roses, 7 February 1995*

chloe.almeras6@orange.fr • 0033 632796151

"IB ROSHI." KALIMAT. SHARJAH. 2016
"IB KHALDON." KALIMAT. SHARJAH. 2016
"MI AMIGA LA ARAÑA." EL FARO. MONTEVIDEO. 2015
"LULU AL LANUDO." EL FARO. MONTEVIDEO. 2015
"PETIT POUCET." BALIVERNES. FRANCHEVILLE. 2015
"YAŞLI ODUNCU ILE TILKI." CAN ÇOCUK. ISTANBUL. 2015
"DER ROLLENDE KÜRBIS." SCHIBRI VERLAG. UCKERLAND. 2014
"OISELLE CORBEAU." GRANDIR. NÎMES. 2012
"SHAHNAMEH STORIES." KHANEYE ADABIYAT. 2012
"EL OSO QUE JAMÁS HABÍA PROBADO LA MIEL." CIDCLI. CIUDAD DE MÉXICO. 2010
"CAJA DE CARTÓN." OQO EDITORA. PONTEVEDRA. 2010
"CHAPO-TUYO." GRANDIR. NÎMES. 2009

"LITTLE RED CAP." EDIÇÕES ÉTEROGÉMEAS. PORTO. 2009

2 THE LITTLE SHIP AND THE GIRL   3 THE GIRL IN THE CABIN ON THE SHIP

4 THE GIRL OPENS THE DOOR TO LEAVE THE LITTLE SHIP   5 FLYING THE LITTLE SHIP TO THE BEACH

HASSAN AMEKAN

The Little Ship • Mixed media • Fiction

Iran • *Astaneh Ashrafiyeh, 21 March 1977*

hassan.amekan@gmail.com • 0098 9331481186

"UN LIBRO SULLE BALENE," CORRAINI EDIZIONI, MANTOVA, 2016
"QUESTO È UN ALCE?," CORRAINI EDIZIONI, MANTOVA, 2015

4

ANDREA ANTINORI
ANDREANTINORI.COM

Trasporti pubblici (Public Transport)

Graphite, colored pencils, acrylic • Fiction

Italy • *Recanati, 17 March 1992*

andreantinori1@gmail.com • 0039 3472391241

1

1 WAITING FOR THE BUS   2 THE BUS   4 THE TAXIS

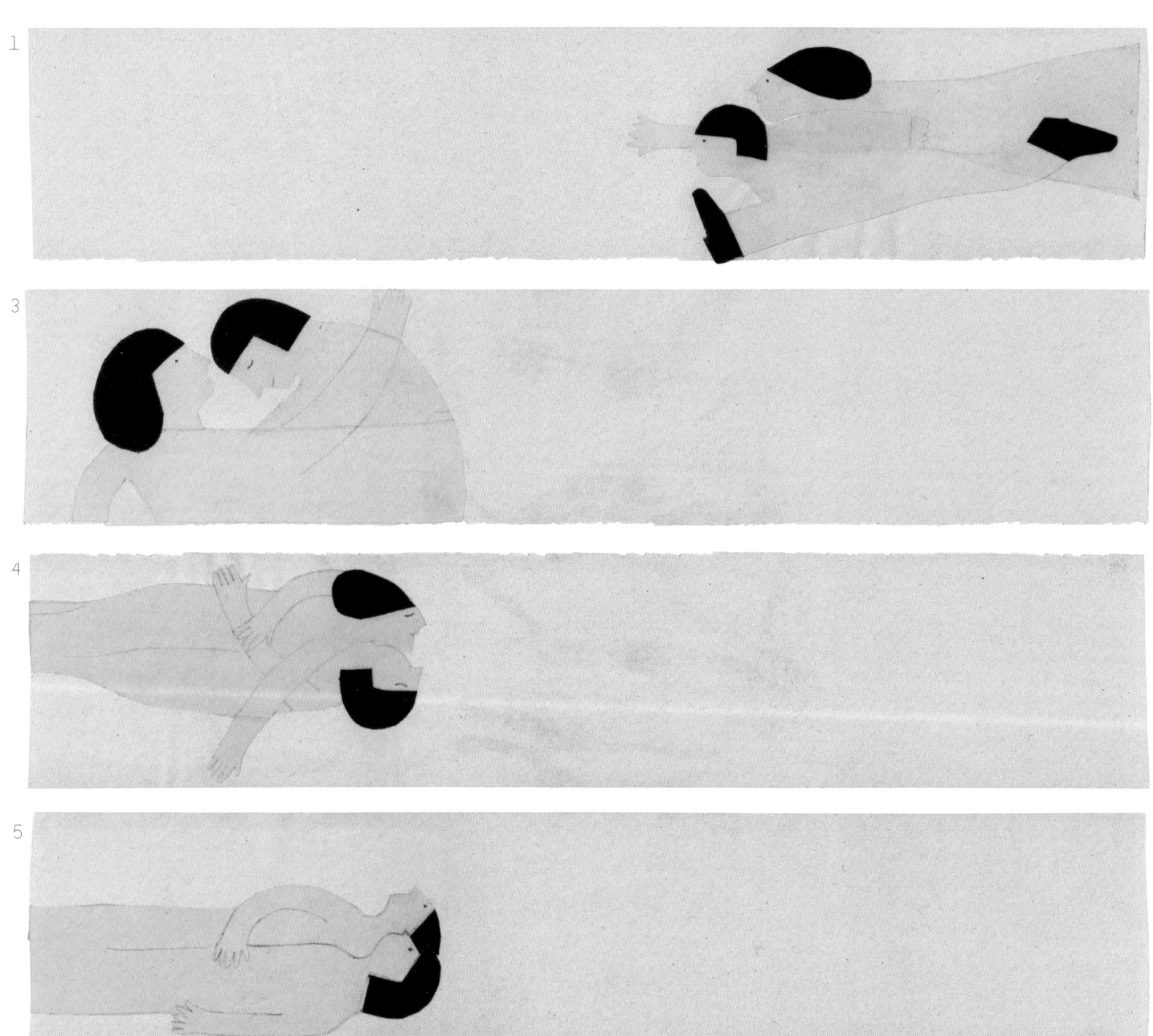

2

MARIA CHIARA ARESTI

MARIACHIARAARESTI.TUMBLR.COM

The Elopement • Collage, tape • Fiction

Italy • *Umbertide, 6 June 1975*

mariach.aresti@tiscali.it • 0039 3332396042

3

"VERSOS DE LA TIERRA." SM. MADRID. 2016
"DIEZ GOTITAS DE AZAR." PERIPLO EDICIONES. BUENOS AIRES. 2016
"HARA!." PAMIELA. NAVARRA. 2012

1

2

4

5

1 IN THE WOODS   2 IN THE LAKE   3 BY NIGHT   4 IN THE CAVE   5 BACK HOME

MIREN ASIAIN LORA

MIASLO.COM

Recuerdo en aquel campamento (Memories of that Camp) • Gouache • Fiction

Spain • *Pamplona, 23 August 1988*

misiain@hotmail.com • 0054 1126514750

1

"DÉCEMBRE." SARBACANE. PARIS. TO BE PUBLISHED IN 2017
"LA LAISSE." MÉMO EDITIONS. NANTES. TO BE PUBLISHED IN 2017

5

MARION BARRAUD

Untitled • Watercolor, pencil • Fiction

France • *Nantes, 30 September 1987*

marion.barraud@gmail.com • 0033-637962400

1

2

44   "J'AIME." L'AGRUME. PARIS. 2015
"IL ÉTAIT PLUSIEURS FOIS." L'ATELIER DU POISSON SOLUBLE. PUY-EN-VELAY. 2014
"BONHOMME. SA MAISON. ET PLUIE ET PLUIE." L'AGRUME. PARIS. 2013

3

5

1 ARCHÌ IS NOT HARLEQUIN   2 HE DOESN'T KNOW HIMSELF THAT HE IS ARCHÌ

5 HE KNOWS THAT. SOMETIMES. THE WIND BLOWS IN A FLASH

3 HE KNOWS THAT. STEP BY STEP. HE WALKS A LITTLE

Archì • Stencils, digital media, stamps • Fiction

Topipittori, Milan, 2015, ISBN 9788898523214

France • *Vitry-sur-Seine, 30 October 1974*

manubastien@gmail.com • 0033 687792583

EMMANUELLE BASTIEN

EMMANUELLEBASTIEN.ULTRA-BOOK.COM

1

2

4

5

3

5 HOLDING MY HAND   4 BUILDING SHIPS   3 AT SATURDAY'S MARKET   2 HIM READING   1 HIS FACE

Forgotten Memories

Ink separation and digital composition • Fiction

Spain • *Barcelona, 11 April 1990*

esther.bernal.lopez@gmail.com • 0034 639760137

ESTHER BERNAL

WWW.ESTHERBERNAL.COM

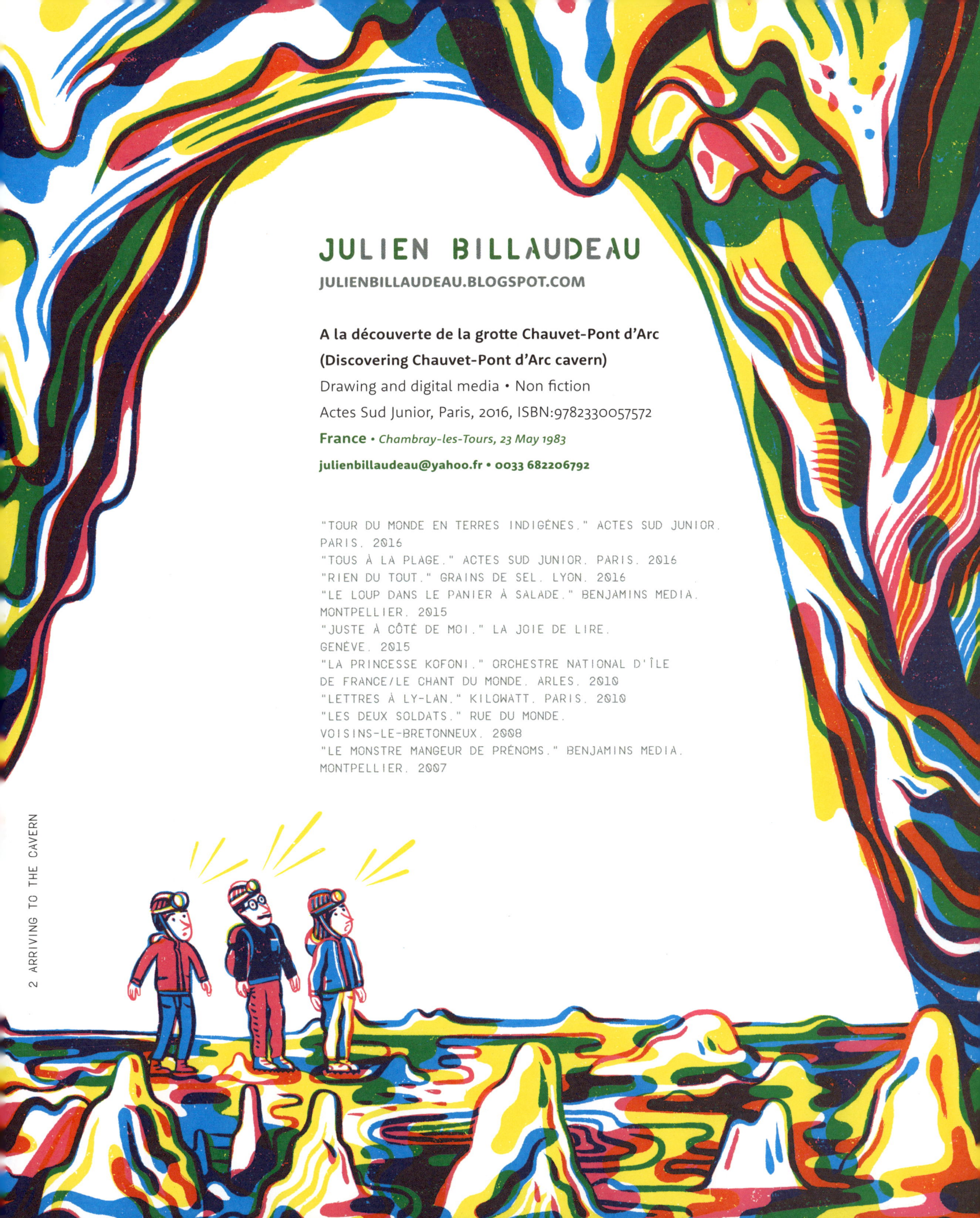

JULIEN BILLAUDEAU

JULIENBILLAUDEAU.BLOGSPOT.COM

A la découverte de la grotte Chauvet-Pont d'Arc
(Discovering Chauvet-Pont d'Arc cavern)
Drawing and digital media • Non fiction
Actes Sud Junior, Paris, 2016, ISBN:9782330057572

France • *Chambray-les-Tours, 23 May 1983*

julienbillaudeau@yahoo.fr • 0033 682206792

"TOUR DU MONDE EN TERRES INDIGÉNES." ACTES SUD JUNIOR.
PARIS. 2016
"TOUS À LA PLAGE." ACTES SUD JUNIOR. PARIS. 2016
"RIEN DU TOUT." GRAINS DE SEL. LYON. 2016
"LE LOUP DANS LE PANIER À SALADE." BENJAMINS MEDIA.
MONTPELLIER. 2015
"JUSTE À CÔTÉ DE MOI." LA JOIE DE LIRE.
GENÉVE. 2015
"LA PRINCESSE KOFONI." ORCHESTRE NATIONAL D'ÎLE
DE FRANCE/LE CHANT DU MONDE. ARLES. 2010
"LETTRES À LY-LAN." KILOWATT. PARIS. 2010
"LES DEUX SOLDATS." RUE DU MONDE.
VOISINS-LE-BRETONNEUX. 2008
"LE MONSTRE MANGEUR DE PRÉNOMS." BENJAMINS MEDIA.
MONTPELLIER. 2007

2 ARRIVING TO THE CAVERN

"PEQUEÑOS GRANDES GESTOS POR EL PLANETA." ALBA EDITORIAL. BARCELONA, 2016

2

4

5

ANA BUSTELO

WWW.ANABUSTELO.ES

Serie B (B Series)

Acrylic, wax pastels and digital media • Fiction

Spain • *Palencia, 13 August 1982*

hola@anabustelo.es • **0034 636467596**

3

ALICE COPPINI
CARGOCOLLECTIVE.COM/ALICECOPPINI

Story of Billie • Gouache and pencils • Non fiction

Italy • *Novara, 28 March 1991*

alice@alicecoppini.it • 0039 3493168648

1

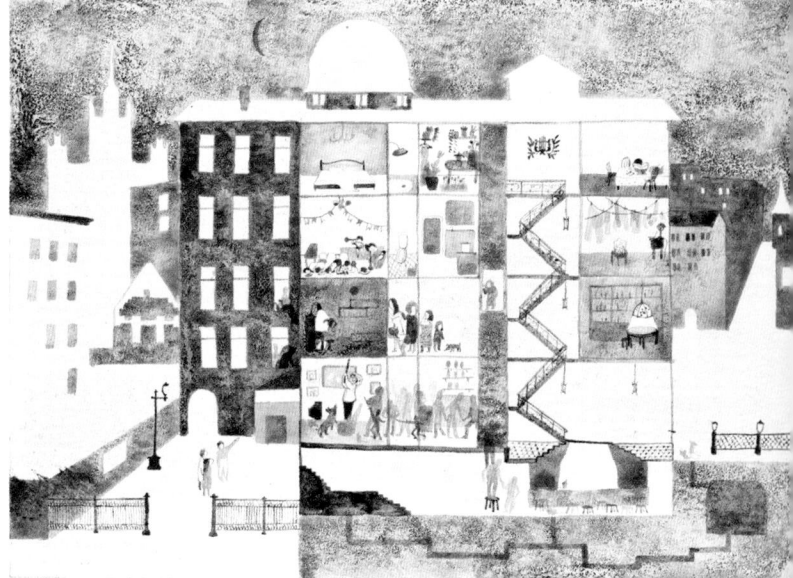

2

3

5

KASYA DENISEVICH

KASYADENISEVICH.COM

Neighbours • Ink on paper • Fiction

Russia • *Moscow, 10 December 1984*

kdenisevich@gmail.com • 0034 634074355, 0079 857657340

"LA GIARA." RAUM ITALIC. BERLIN. 2015

Che spavento/Oh schreck! (What a scare!) • Digital media • Fiction
Raum Italic/Spazio Corsivo, Berlin, 2016, ISBN 9783944858241
Italy • *Pescara, 7 December 1982*
lucadibat@gmail.com • 0049 15155218510

LUCA DI BATTISTA
WWW.LUCADIBATTISTA.COM

1

2

3

4

"EGGHEAD." ELI READERS. RECANATI. 2016
"STO NÓG STONOGI FRUZI." DWIE SIOSTRY. WARSZAWA. 2015
58 "A TESTA IN GIÚ." TOPIPITTORI. MILANO. 2014

ZOSIA DZIERŻAWSKA
WWW.ZOZOZOSIA.COM

A Piece of String • Ink, colored pencils • Non fiction

Poland • *Warszawa, 22 April 1983*

contact@zozozosia.com • 0048 501214606

STELLENBOSCH UNIVERSITY
DIRECTOR: ELIZABETH GUNTER
COORDINATOR: MARTHIE KADEN

LENÉ EHLERS
WWW.INSTAGRAM.COM/LENEEHLERS/

Nothing is really clear and they don't know what they are doing
Gouache, ink and collage • Fiction
Republic of South Africa • *Cape Town, 28 March 1994*
lene.el.ehlers@gmail.com • 0027 846759218

she loves it WHEN THE CHAIR

doesn't BREAK when someone sits on it

ONe TiMe SHe MaDe A CHaiR iNSPiReD By A

and launched it AT oNe of THe ROYaL HoT DoG CLub's NoTORiOUS PaRTies...

4

2

Роберт очень любит осень, запах сухой жухлой травы, пронзительный ветер и тяжелые сине-сизые тучи

3

Роберт часто приходит на холодный пустынный берег садится на сырую траву и смотрит на море

4

У Роберта
есть добрый
друг. Он
живёт в доми-
ке у озера
сейчас Роберт его
позовёт
гулять и
падаваться
ЛЕСУ!

5

Друзья не
заметили
как стало
вечереть.
Пошел снег.
Они замёрзли
вконец и побе-
жали на свет
в окошке, про-
ситься на
чай, погреться

OLGA EZOVA-DENISOVA

EZOVADENISOVA.RU

Robert the Wolf and his Autumn • Textile collage, embroidery • Fiction

Russia • Yekaterinburg, 15 March 1983

ezovadenisova@gmail.com • 007 9126855569

"I PICCOLINI E I MOSTRI DEL PARCO." ED. EINAUDI. TRIESTE. 2007
"IL FEROCE SALATINO." EDIZIONI EL. TRIESTE. 2007
"LA SOLITA STORIA DI ANIMALI?." MUP EDITORE. COPRODOTTO DAL FESTIVAL
DI LETTERATURA PER L'INFANZIA MINIMONDI. PARMA. 2006
"IO E LA TIGRE." SINNOS. ROMA. 2003
"IN VOLO - ANTOLOGIA PER LA SCUOLA MEDIA." ZANICHELLI. BOLOGNA. 2003
"L'OEIL AMUSÉ: LE CORPS." EDITIONS DU ROUERGUE. ARLES. 2002
"MASCHERE." CITTÀ NUOVA EDITRICE. ROMA. 2001

1

2

3

4

1 KNIGHT POUËT-POUËT 2 KNIGHT KADORLA-BAGARRE 5 KNIGHT PLIK-PLOK
4 KNIGHT MILOS-DU-POULET
3 KNIGHT KURT-PATTE

100 chevaliers au secours de la princesse

(100 Knights to Rescue the Princess) • Digital media • Fiction

Éditions Amaterra, Lyon, 2016, ISBN 9782368560983

CAMILLA FALSINI

CAMILLAFALSINI.IT

Italy • *Rome, 12 December 1975*

io@camillafalsini.it • 0039 3402912201

Starting from the thousands of illustrations you have examined over the last few days, do differences still exist regarding styles, techniques and imagery in different geographical or cultural areas, or is illustration becoming increasingly global and across-the-board?

I have the impression that illustration is getting more and more global and universal, so that the imagery, styles and techniques wind up blending together in a path that not only allows for movement in two directions, but also often opens up curious crossroads. It is precisely thanks to these intersections that the person who illustrates, if equipped with boundless curiosity and a sufficiently deep reserve of intuition, can run the risk of digging up and developing original associations.

Are there differences between a good illustrator and a good illustrator for children?

The differences exist in the audience that views the images, in the context in which they are developed, but not so much in the creative process. Yes, there is a difference in relation to the cultural references that can give meaning to an image, but beyond this particular factor, I believe the creative process follows similar paths in both cases. Then there are artists whose work is aimed at children or at adults in a more natural way, but this has to do with the centers of interest, with the language a person uses for expression.

Do you believe that children's books can also approach problematic themes like war, death or illness?

Can they? They have to. Children's books, as works of literature, tell stories that talk about life, so they have to address everything that is a part of life. War, death and illness are part of life. Literature does not hide, does not deny, it investigates and delves deeper. After all, a human being, a "polytropic," many-sided Ulyssian human being, cannot avoid asking questions and finding interest in everything that happens around him. Actually, if we consider children's books as literary and artistic works, I don't think we should even be asking this question. The problem arises when the book becomes a tool of transmission of commonly accepted values, and of a lifestyle. Then, if we decide to include themes that are considered complicated, it is done in a rigid way. But works of this type, though they present themselves physically in the form of a book, cannot be considered literature, nor are they scientifically or philosophically interesting.

How can an editor help an illustrator while working on an illustrated book?

An editor's role is to make an illustrator's book the best possible version of itself while

JUROR
**POINT
OF VIEW
HARRIET
BIRKINSHAW**

also ensuring the illustrator's vision is clear to the reader. We give lots of support, suggestions and advice. Making a book can be a daunting process, and having an editor to support you or be used as a sounding board can help with the process. With illustrated books in particular, we also look at how the text and illustrations complement each other. There should be a wonderful synthesis between the two.

Are we going through a resurgence of illustrated non-fiction children's books? How is this phenomenon shaping children's illustration?

Yes. It is opening up opportunities for illustrators whose styles are more suited to non-fiction topics. Children's illustration is steeped in tradition and sometimes in the past that has been limiting. The wider illustration community is much more diverse, and now we are seeing all sorts of styles and techniques being used in children's illustration, which is exciting.

How has social media changed the relationship between illustrators and publishers?

It is a matter of exposure. It is now much easier to see all kinds of styles by illustrators all over the world. There are many online communities that publishers can access. Recently I discovered a website called "Women Who Draw" that is a brilliant directory of various female illustrators.

Is the market a force that tends to homogenize and standardize the work of illustrators, or is it a necessary space of exchange between the authors' creativity and the readers' tastes?

I think it works both ways. There are always trends and certain taste guidelines that illustrators tend to follow in order to give the market what it needs and find work.

On the other hand, the market can be also a platform where innovative work can find its place and reshape the readers' tastes at the same time. Of course that creates a circle: innovative art becomes a trend, then illustrators follow it until something new comes along.

What is the difference between creating a single picture and illustrating an entire book? What is your relationship with the text when creating illustrations for a book?

Creating a book means that all the illustrations must have continuity, rhythm, narration, a sense of unity between them; a story has to be told by the same hand, but each illustration represents just one piece of the story. A single picture may be easier because it doesn't have to relate to other images, but it does have to be a carrier of a deeper, more to-the-point idea. My relationship varies, depending on the text.

What is the best advice you have received as an illustrator?

This advice I received as a painter, but it goes also for illustrating: before finishing a piece of art, give it a rest for a few days. Then you will be able to give it the finishing touch or detect what is wrong with it, and make it right. If possible, don't give it away before you do that.

"BOMBO," TIAN'AN, CHINA

CANDELA FERDMANN

CFILUSTRACIONES.BLOGSPOT.COM.AR

My Red Round Piece of Fruit • Watercolor, digital media • Fiction

Argentina • *Mar del Plata, 10 October 1980*

candelaferdmann@yahoo.com.ar • 0054 1148216276

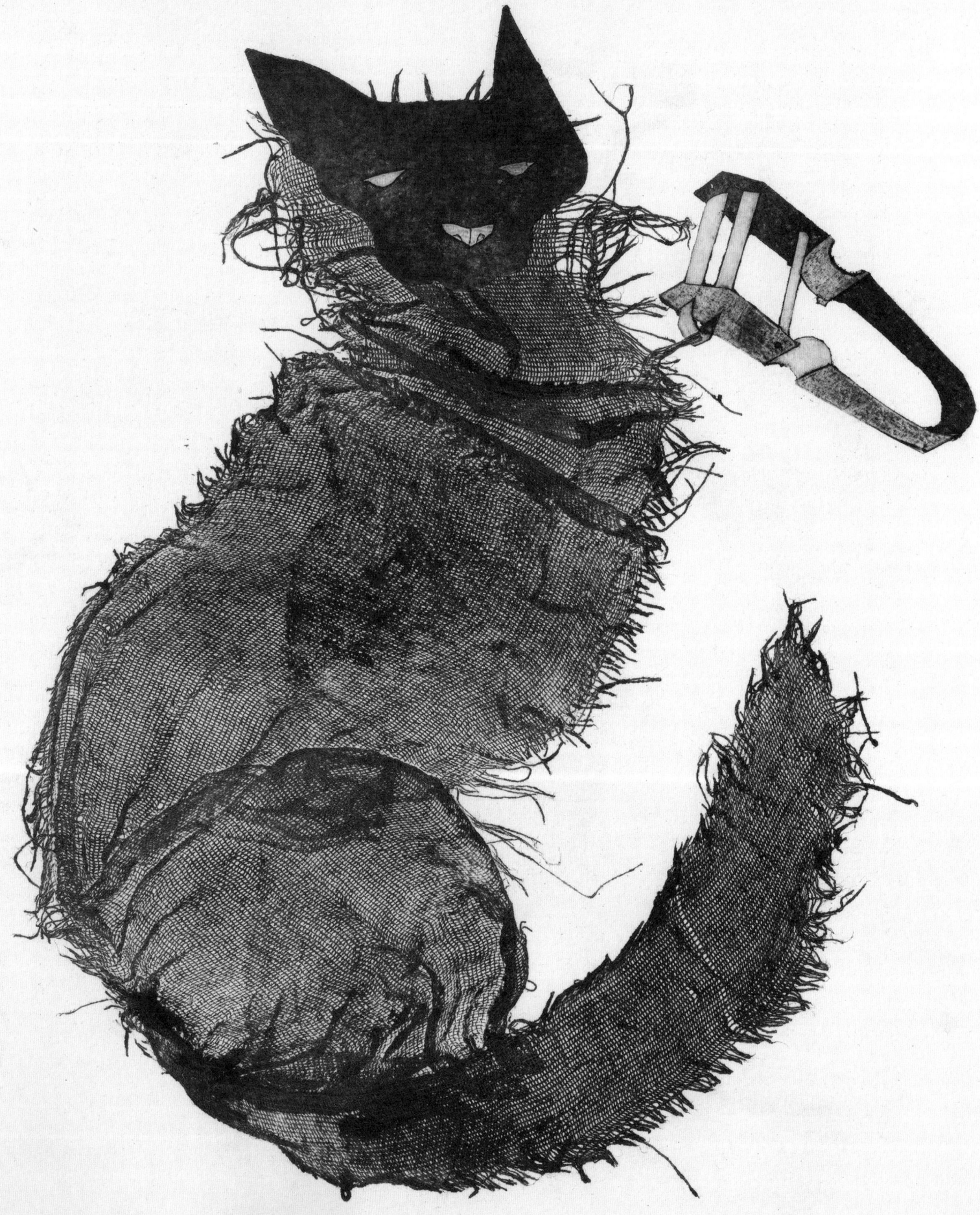

ACCADEMIA DI BELLE ARTI DI BOLOGNA
DIRECTOR: ENRICO FORNAROLI
COORDINATOR: ALESSANDRO SANNA

CECILIA FERRI

CECILIAFERRI.COM

Animali da dire (Animals to Say)

Experimental copperplate engraving techniques • Fiction

Italy • *Forlimpopoli, 17 January 1992*

cecilia.ferri1@gmail.com • 0039 3291876697

1 CRAZY LIKE A HORSE   5 QUANDARY CAT

1

"MALA SUERTE/QUELLE CHANCE!." LA JOIE DE LIRE.
GENÈVE. TO BE PUBLISHED
"HUERTA." AMANUTA. SANTIAGO DE CHILE. 2016
"UN HUECO." CALIBROSCOPIO. BUENOS AIRES. 2015
"A SIMPLE VISTA." AMANUTA. SANTIAGO DE CHILE. 2014
"NIENTE DI NIENTE." KITE EDIZIONI/PASSEPARTOUT.
PIAZZOLA SUL BRENTA (PD). 2014

1

5

4

YAEL FRANKEL
YAELFRANKEL.COM

Carousel • Stamps and digital media • Fiction

Argentina • *Buenos Aires, 10 September 1967*

yaelfrankel@hotmail.com • 0054 91168466168

2

3

4

5

1 I HAVE A MEETING AT THE STATUE   2 I AM HAVING A CUP OF COFFEE IN THE TEA ROOM   3 I AM GOING HOME AFTER SHOPPING   4 ON THE WAY HOME. I STOP AT THE PUBLIC BATHS   5 IT'S LATE AT NIGHT. WE ARE DRINKING BEER

KANAKO FURUGORI

FURUGORIKANAKO.WIXSITE.COM/FURUGORIKANAKO

One day • Acrylic paint • Fiction

Japan • *Tokyo, 15 November 1985*

furugorikanako@hotmail.co.jp • 0081 9029121750

1 BIRTHDAY ICE CREAM TASTES LIKE WRAPPERS. STICKY KISSES AND BLOWN-OUT CANDLES 3 FIRST DAY OF SCHOOL ICE CREAM TASTES LIKE PENCIL SHAVINGS. BLANK PAPER AND NEW CLOTHES 4 DENTIST ICE CREAM TASTES LIKE MINT. WAITING AND ALCOHOL 5 DARKNESS ICE CREAM TASTES LIKE BLANKETS. MONSTER EYES AND MYSTERY

CATERINA GABELLI & SARA MARAGOTTO
STUDIOFLUDD.COM

An Ice Cream a Day • Collage • Fiction

Italy • *Padova, 18 October 1984*   **Italy** • *Padova, 7 October 1986*

caterina@studiofludd.com • 0039 3334003185   sara@studiofludd.com • 0039 3334003185

1

2

3

4

MONICA HERNANDEZ

MONICAHERNANDEZJ.BLOGSPOT.IT

Biancaneve e i sette nani
(Snow White and the Seven Dwarfs)

Graphite and colored pencils • Fiction

Italy • *La Habana, 5 July 1980*

monicahernandezj@gmail.com • 0039 3281567879

1

3

4

5

1 SPORTS GYM   2 APARTMENT   3 NARROW PATH   4 COMMUNITY CENTER   5 RAMP

AYANO HONDA

Koala's Commuting Time • Pencil, gouache, collage • Fiction

Japan • *Kumamoto, 12 November 1985*

ayanohonda.work@gmail.com

1

2

3

1 ONE TROMBONE PLAYED   2 THE TROMBONE AND A TRUMPET PLAYED. THAT WAS TWO   3 THE TROMBONE. THE TRUMPET AND A HORN PLAYED. THAT WAS THREE   4 THE TROMBONE. THE TRUMPET. THE HORN AND A CELLO PLAYED. THAT WAS FOUR

YEON GYONG JOO
YEON-GYONG.BLOGSPOT.IT

Orchestra 123 • Risograph print, ink pen and digital media • Fiction

Korea • *Seoul, 22 February 1976*

yeongyongjoo@gmail.com • 0082 1032373295

"THE YOUNG FELLOW & THE CUNNING TAILOR." KANOON. TEHRAN. 2008
"ARANG. ARANG. TELL ME WHAT COLOR IS IT?." KANOON. TEHRAN. 2008
"MAHTITI AND KOLAHTITI." KANOON. TEHRAN. 2006
"THE RED BALL." KANOON. TEHRAN. 2005
"THE DOG WHO CROAKED." KANOON. TEHRAN

1

5

2

1 THE LITTLE BOY GETS ONTO THE TRAIN WITH HIS BIRD IN A CAGE   3 THE OLD MAN IN THE PARK TRIES
2 THE BIRD FLIES AWAY THROUGH AN OPEN WINDOW OF THE TRAIN   5 KIDS SHOWING OFF WITH THEIR BIRDS BY THE LITTLE BOY'S HOUSE
TO WHISTLE FOR THE BIRDS

RASHIN KHEIRIYEH
RASHINART.COM

Boy, Train and Bird • Mixed media • Fiction

Iran • *Khoramshahr, 26 September 1979*

rashinart@yahoo.com • 001 2028137243

AUSRA KIUDULAITE

Laimė yra lapė (Happiness is a Fox)

Mixed media: digital media, paper cut-outs • Fiction

Tikra Knyga, Vilnius, 2016, ISBN 9786098142310

Lithuania • *Vilnius, 16 April 1978*

kiudulaitei@gmail.com • 00370 861838934

2

3

4

5

1 YOU TURN ON THE POWER SWITCHES. THEN YOU SEE.... 2 AN ELEPHANT WORKING TO KEEP THE CITY CLEAN 3 A LION GETTING HUNGRY AT THE NOISY STATION SQUARE 4 A BIRD MAKING A WHIRRING SOUND ON THE BEACH 5 A GIRAFFE STUDYING HARD AT NIGHT IN THE PARK

TOYOHIKO KOKUMAI

Travel of Electricity • Collage • Fiction

Japan • *Hyogo, 2 March 1956*

gingerlei-5901@skyblue.ocn.ne.jp • 0081 788412992

4

"IMAGEM." PLANETA TANGERINA. CARCAVELOS. 2016
"TRAVALENGAS A DOBRAR." BOOKSMILE. AMADORA. 2016
"GATO PROCURA-SE." CAMINHO. ALFRAGIDE. 2015
"ABZZZZ..." PLANETA TANGERINA. CARCAVELOS. 2014
"QUADRINHAS." EDITORA 34. SÃO PAULO. 2014
"RIMAS DE LÁ E DE CÁ." PEIRÓPOLIS. SÃO PAULO. 2014
"UMA ONDA PEQUENINA." PLANETA TANGERINA. CARCAVELOS. 2013
"TANTOS ANIMAIS E OUTRAS LENGALENGAS DE CONTAR." PLANETA TANGERINA. CARCAVELOS. 2013
"EM CIMA DAQUELA SERRA." COMPANHIA DAS LETRINHAS. SÃO PAULO. 2013
"O TESOURO DO PALÁCIO." CAMINHO. ALFRAGIDE. 2012
"A ILHA. PLANETA TANGERINA." CARCAVELOS. 2012
"PIRILAMPOS E ESTRELAS." APCC. LISBOA. 2011
"COMO É QUE UMA GALINHA..." PLANETA TANGERINA. CARCAVELOS. 2011
"EU SÓ - SÓ EU." CAMINHO. ALFRAGIDE. 2011
"O AR ESTÁ CHEIO DE VOZES." CAMINHO. ALFRAGIDE. 2011
"A MANTA." PLANETA TANGERINA. CARCAVELOS. 2010
"O PAPÃO NO DESVÃO." CAMINHO. ALFRAGIDE. 2010
"OVELHINHA DÁ-ME LÃ." KALANDRAKA. PONTEVEDRA. 2010
"DE SOL A SONHO." CAMINHO. ALFRAGIDE. 2009

YARA KONO

YARAKONO.BLOGSPOT.IT

Batata chaca-chaca (Chaca-chaca potato) • Mixed media, digital editing • Fiction
Planeta Tangerina, Carcavelos, 2016, ISBN 9789898145765

Portugal • *São Paulo, 1 November 1972*

yara.kono@planetatangerina.com•00351 961939661

1
2

"MENINO SEMENTE." MOV PALABRAS. SÃO PAULO. 2014
"A FLORESTA ÍRIS." MOV PALABRAS. SÃO PAULO. 2014
"SE EU FOSSE UMA ÀRVORE." GAIVOTA. SÃO PAULO. 2012
"RIMAS FÀCEIS." GAIVOTA. SÃO PAULO. 2012
"A CALOROSA AVENTURA." JBC. SÃO PAULO. 2012
"DO MUNDO AO FUNDO DO FUNDO AO MUNDO." JBC. SÃO PAULO. 2011
"OS ÓCULOS DO LEÃO." LCTE. SÃO PAULO. 2010

FACULDADE DE BELAS ARTES DA UNIVERSIDADE DO PORTO. PORTUGAL
DIRECTOR: JOSÉ CARLOS DE PAIVA E SILVA

3

4

TALITA NOZOMI KUSUNOKI
TALITANOZOMI.COM

Pelas Lentes de Mel e Leo (Through the Lenses of Mel and Leo)

Mixed media: colored pencils, photographs, collage • Fiction

Brazil • *São Paulo, 11 August 1985*

talitanozomi@gmail.com • 00351 913148416

MYUNGAE LEE
MYUNGAELEE.COM

Yellow line • Watercolor, pencil, digital media • Fiction
Korea • *Seoul, 24 November 1976*
reinvest@naver.com • **0082 1099754149**

1 THE YELLOW LINE BECOMES A SUBWAY 3 AND ALSO IT BECOMES THE STAIRS

1

2 PIG. ON THE CARPET. PIG. BENEATH THE CARPET / PIG. BENEATH THE CARPET / PIG. ON THE CARPET. PIG. ON THE CARPET 5 PIGS. MANY? / PIGS. A FEW

Opposite Pigs (relativity)
Print, paper ironing techniques (lacquer thinner) • Non fiction
Bandal Publishing, Seoul, ISBN 9788956187273 77810

SOON OK LEE
Korea • *Hwaseong, 25 August 1971*
flowand@naver.com • 0082 1067440516

CONTINUED ON PAGE

2

4

5

EMMA LEWIS

EMMA-LEWIS.CO.UK

The Museum of Me

Mixed media: collage and digital color • Fiction

Tate Publishing, London, 2016, ISBN 9781849764148

United Kingdom • *London, 12 February 1988*

emma@emma-lewis.co.uk • **0044 7847570507**

JUROR
**POINT
OF VIEW
JEAN-
FRANÇOIS
MARTIN**

What's more important for an illustrator: technique or a personal style?

I think there is a fragile balance between these two aspects, and something more. An illustration can be simple, or very graphic, and still be of great quality; or it can be extremely painstaking, generous, almost exaggerated, and also be perfect. I believe the objective and the way the work relates to the text are the truly important factors. Two illustrators can do a completely different job on the same text and both, in any case, achieve excellent results.

What are the three fundamental qualities for a good illustrator of children's books?

There are so many perspectives on illustration that I find it very hard to name three fundamental qualities for an illustrator. The works of Roberto Innocenti and those of Jean-Jacques Sempé are literally opposites, they do not require the same skills, but they are still magnificent.

When you work on a book for children or teenagers do you have an image of your ideal reader in mind?

I never think about the readers. I work egotistically, with the goal of getting as much pleasure as possible. But my daughters keep an eye on me, and always bring me back into line. If they do not understand the image, or if they simply don't like it, I usually correct it to match their tastes.

Amidst thousands of drawings, styles and very different techniques, how does one select a good illustration?

I'm not very interested in "good" illustration. I'm much more interested in exciting illustration, surprising illustration, strange illustration.

Illustrations, at their most functionally basic, must fulfill the purpose for which they were created: must be appropriate. Illustrations, unlike art created for gallery walls, have a job to do.

But a truly surprising illustration can utterly alter the context for which it was created. A surprising illustration can make you read the article it was drawn for in a new way. On the cover, it can set the mood for a book. And it can transform a simple (perhaps even ordinary) picture book text into a visual poem, an exercise in wonder.

So when I'm confronted by an ocean of illustrative images, as I was during the jurying of the Illustrators' Exhibition, or on a daily basis, as I scroll and page through the amazing and at times overwhelming number of illustrations that greet us daily in print and on our digital devices, rather than appraising an image for its style or technical bravura, I'm looking for an internal response: delight, stupefaction, envy ("I wish I'd drawn that!") or excitement at the discovery of a freshly minted visual idea. These are responses elicited by only a handful of images.

For an illustrator, is having a clearly recognizable style a necessity, or is it also a prison, in a certain sense?

Illustration isn't really a unitary field. There's illustration for magazines and newspapers, for advertising, for corporate clients, comics and graphic novels, and of course for children's books. Within illustration for children's books alone there are a variety of needs.

Versatility has at times been considered a liability in illustration. It seemed to indicate an artist who had no strong personal identity, no single expressive voice. "Jack of all trades" was not a term of approbation, and yet some of the most influential and protean artists were and are remarkably versatile, able to speak in many voices, none seemingly inauthentic. Artists like Pablo Picasso in the fine arts and Seymour Chwast in design and illustration exemplify that model.

Some artists believe that their work should serve the purpose to which it's put and shift their work accordingly, that to have one way of doing things is foolish, if not unprofessional. And then there are, of course, those artists whose way of working has changed, either organically or explosively, over time. Think of the painter Philip Guston's paintings in his later years, or the illustrator Philippe Weisbecker, throughout his career. I remember meeting Guy Billout, whom I revered, at the *New York Times* when I was just starting out and was casting about for a means of expression, a visual mode that I could inhabit comfortably and call my own. It seemed that every time I got an assignment I'd try a different identity, a different technique or style: collage, pencil, pen and ink, rubber stamp. I really had no idea what I was doing from one assignment to the next. Guy, on meeting me, said with enthusiasm: "Oh you're the guy who's always experimenting!" I wished I'd had the confidence to experiment. I was really just looking for one way to work that I could latch onto and repeat until my pen dropped in old age. Certainly, when editorial illustration was one of the most common and lucrative areas of creative activity, when hundreds of daily newspapers and weekly and monthly magazines used upwards of twenty illustrations each issue, there was a purely commercial value in having a recognizable visual language. Art directors had tremendous creative control over their publications' visual environment and having a distinct voice that spoke to the art director was essential. Of course, when print media began to decline and magazines and newspapers began to fold, being able to suit many different clients' needs with many different styles of expression meant simply economic survival.

Children's books seem to me to be much more impervious to these vagaries in the market. In books, the ability to create strong narrative imagery that conveys strong ideas is paramount. Either expressing oneself in one voice, or being a visual polyglot are equally valued, as long as one's ideas are fresh and fluently expressed in whatever visual language one speaks.

How is the spread of digital techniques and formats changing illustration?
Technique is really immaterial when appraising illustrations. A stark image scrawled with a stick dipped in ink can be as rivetingly effective (and sometimes more so) than a beautifully layered image that deploys all of the brushes and filters that the digital toolkit provides to the contemporary artist. The illustration's surface is only one aspect of what makes an image compelling.

That said, on a professional level, new technologies have shifted the creative conversation between artist and art director or editor, and between the artist and him or herself. The digital image is, in a sense, constantly in flux, never truly fixed.

The ability to change an illustration quickly and easily gives the artist much more flexibility to try various colors and styles of mark-making in the creation of an image. Compositional decisions are much more readily explored and discarded. This is a boon for the artist but also a bane—this ease can encourage an art director's unconfident capricious change of mind. Beginning with the introduction of the fax as the standard means to present roughs, the new speed with which an image could be created and revised was a development that cut both ways.

Another wholly unforeseen outcome of digital image making is one of scale. When I first came to New York and attended the annual exhibit openings at the Society of Illustrators in the 1970s, the rooms were crisscrossed with temporary walls, which were hung with oil paintings and drawings framed like old masters, as big as anything found at the Metropolitan Museum of Art. In fact, as a pen-and-ink illustrator, and a minimalist at that, I doubted I'd ever see my own work on those walls.

A couple of years ago, having seen my work hung on those same walls for some time and having chaired the annual exhibition, I began to notice that the work in the show was easily accommodated by the permanent walls themselves. No temporary walls needed. Not only that, but most of the work was more or less the same size, approximately 11x17 or sometimes smaller. This at first struck me as odd, until I realized that much of the art was created digitally, and even much of work that was created with traditional media was printed out and framed. The size of the art was dictated by the dimensions of an oversized scanner bed. A certain uniformity of scale was being imposed by the exigencies of digital technology.

"ALDOUS HUXLEY: A VARJAK ÉS A CSÖRGŐKÍGYÓ." KÉT EGÉR KÖNYVEK. BUDAPEST. 2016
"HÉTMADÁR." CD-MELLÉKLETTEL. KOLIBRI KIADÓ. BUDAPEST. 2016
"ÁLLATOK ÁBÉCÉJE." SCOLAR. BUDAPEST. 2015
"THE ABC ZOO." SCOLAR. BUDAPEST. 2015
"KISMADÁR ÉS KÓRÓ DIAFILM. DIAFILMGYÁRTÓ." BUDAPEST. 2015
"KNIGHTS AND CASTLES, ACTIVITY BOOK." THE SALARIYA BOOK COMPANY. BRIGHTON. 2015
"EZ NEM AZ APU HANGJA!" CD-MELLÉKLETTEL. BETŰTÉSZTA KIADÓ. BUDAKESZI. 2015
"LOVAK ÉS LOVASOK." KÉT EGÉR KÖNYVEK. BUDAPEST. 2014
"SZERDA (MERCREDI)." KÉT EGÉR KÖNYVEK. BUDAPEST. 2014
"A JAKIFÉSZEK." SCOLAR. BUDAPEST. 2014
"PTACE A BODLÁK (KISMADÁR ÉS KÓRÓ)." ALBATROS BOOKS. PRÁGA. 2014
"RAPTORMESE DIAFILM." DIAFILMGYÁRTÓ. BUDAPEST. 2014
"RAPTORMESE." KOLIBRI. BUDAPEST. 2014
"JÁRTAMBAN... KERTEMBEN." KÉT EGÉR KÖNYVEK. BUDAPEST. 2013
"A REPÜLÉS TÖRTÉNETE." KÉT EGÉR KÖNYVEK. BUDAPEST. 2013
"INCOLAE MARIUM." KÉT EGÉR KÖNYVEK. BUDAPEST. 2013
"KISMADÁR ÉS KÓRÓ." SCOLAR. BUDAPEST. 2012
"INUIT" (DIPLOMA PROJECT). MOME. BUDAPEST. 2009
"PIRATE ACTIVITY BOOK." THE SALARIYA BOOK COMPANY. BRIGHTON

5

3

4

MARIANN MÁRAY

PIKKUDOT.COM

Utazz bálnabusszal! (Travel with the Whale Bus!)

Acrylic on cardboard • Fiction

Két Egér Könyvek, Budapest, 2017, ISBN 9786158003773

Hungary • *Budapest, 10 June 1978*

regifoxmariann@gmail.com • 0036 709421507

1

4

"VILLA VALMARANA E L'INCANTESIMO DEL VENTO." FONDAZIONE ZAVREL. SARMEDE. 2015
"TERRA TRA LE MANI." ANICIA. ROMA. 2015
"IOLE LA BALENA MANGIAPAROLE." GRIBAUDO. TORINO. 2012
"ZIO VANIA E ALTRE STORIE RUSSE." NUOVE EDIZIONI ROMANE. ROMA. 2012
"PICCOLE DONNE OGGI." NUOVE EDIZIONI ROMANE. ROMA 2012
"FANTAVOLIERI." GRIBAUDO. TORINO. 2011

GIOIA MARCHEGIANI

MARCHEGIANI.COM

Il campanellino d'argento (The Little Silver Bell)
Brush pen, roller pen, marker, collage • Fiction
Topipittori, Milan, 2017, ISBN 9788898523726

Italy • *Rome, 22 April 1972*
gioia@marchegiani.com • 0039 3383027794

1 ONCE UPON A TIME THERE WAS AN ISLAND FULL OF STONES. BUSHES AND TREES 4 THUS THE DREAM OF A HOUSE FULL OF ROOFS. AND ROOMS OVERLOOKING THE VALLEY TAKES FORM INSIDE HIM 5 HE PLAYS AND PLAYS. HE PLAYS SO MUCH THAT IN THE END MUSIC IS BORN INSIDE HIM

HER SPLENDID GARDEN AND A VEGETABLE PATCH WHERE PLANTS MINGLE WITH FLOWERS

4 SPIDERS DESCENDED FROM THE HIGH BRANCHES LIKE STARS

ELENA MARICONE

ELENAMARICONE.BLOGSPOT.IT

Oltre il muro (Beyond the Wall) • Monotype, stencils, stamps • Fiction

Italy • *Savona, 26 November 1981*

elena.maricone@gmail.com • 0039 3920572126

1

2

"A MINHA CIDADE: MADRID." PATO LÓGICO EDICÕES. LISBON. 2017
"EL GATO DE BRASIL." EKARÉ. BARCELONA. 2016
"LA VENUS DE LAS PIELES." SEXTO PISO. MADRID. 2016
"O TEMPO DO GIGANTE." ORFEU NEGRO. LISBON. 2015
"LA METAMORFOSIS." ASTRO REY. BARCELONA. 2015
"AHAB Y LA BALLENA BLANCA." EDELVIVES. MADRID. 2014

3

4

Strange Mountain • Acrylic, watercolor, gouache,
plastic paint, oil, ink, wax pastels, pencil on wood.
Digital fix of color and levels • Fiction

MANUEL MARSOL
MANUELMARSOL.COM
Spain • Madrid, 28 April 1984
manuelmarsol@gmail.com • 0034 676339483

"PIC DE LA MIRANDOLE ET L'ANGE JALOUX " LE PETITS PLATONS PARIS 2015

1

"STORIES FROM BUG GARDEN." CANDLEWICK. SOMERVILLE. 2016
"THE SNUGGLE SANDWICH." ANDERSEN PRESS. LONDON. 2013
"THE BOG BABY." PUFFIN. LONDON. 2008

"GUESS WHAT I FOUND IN DRAGON WOOD." PUFFIN. LONDON. 2007

GWEN MILLWARD
GWENMILLWARD.ME

Untitled • Chinagraph pencil, pencil, brush pen, pen • Fiction
United Kingdom • *Hitchin, 4 February 1980*
gwenimillward@hotmail.com • 0044 7815736903

1 BIRD FLIES HIGH OVER TALL BUILDINGS   2 BIRD LANDS

"I WAS A DEER." OFOQ. TEHRAN. 2016
"GOOD NIGHT COMMANDER." OFOQ. TEHRAN. 2003
"I DON'T AFRAID." BEHNASHR. TEHRAN
"THE PRINCESS WHO COULDN'T LAUGH." KANOON. TEHRAN

1

2

4

5

1 THREE SCIENTISTS WENT TO THE KING WITH THEIR HANDMADE PRESENTS   2 THE PRINCE RODE A MAGICAL TROJAN HORSE. AND REACHED A BEAUTIFUL COUNTRY   3 WHEN THE PRINCE WAS CLIMBING A LADDER. HE GLIMPSED A BEAUTIFUL GIRL AND FELL IN LOVE WITH HER   4 THE GIRL WAS A PRINCESS. AND THEY FELL IN LOVE WITH EACH OTHER   5 THE PRINCE WONDERED HOW HE COULD FIGHT ALONE AGAINST THE HUGE ARMY OF A KING

One Thousand and One Nights (Trojan Horse)

Collage, monoprint, pencil, pen • Fiction

NARGES MOHAMMADI

NARGESMOHAMMADI.BLOGSPOT.COM

Iran • *Arak, 30 July 1978*

narsisus_moh@yahoo.com • 0098 9125476250

 PATO LÓGICO PUBLISHING HOUSE

MARTA MONTEIRO

MARTAMONTEIRO.COM

Ana de Castro Osório: the woman who voted in literature • Mixed media • Non fiction

Pato Lógico / Imprensa Nacional - Casa da Moeda (co-edition), Lisbon, 2015, ISBN 9789722723343

Portugal • *Penafiel, 15 February 1973*

martamonteir@gmail.com • 00351 961620643

1

2

HAW HAMBURG
DIRECTOR: CLAUS-DIETER WACKER
122 COORDINATOR: JENNY KAHLER

3

5

PAULINE MUNIQUE
BEHANCE.NET/PAULINEMUNIQUE

Tel Aviv is What You See — Hummus for My Eyes

Acrylic and pencil drawing • Non fiction

Germany • *Lörrach, 19 July 1990*

p.munique@posteo.de • **0049 17657913603**

1

2.

3

4

MAYUMI OONO
O-ONO.JP

Color & Pattern · Digital media · Non fiction

Japan · *Tokyo, 6 April 1975*

hello@o-ono.jp · 0081 9085006577

"ESTABA LA RANA." EDICIONES EKARÉ. BARCELONA. 2015
"UN PERRO EN CASA." EDICIONES EKARÉ. BARCELONA. 2012
"UN ABUELO. SÍ." EDICIONES EKARÉ. BARCELONA. 2011
"AMIGO ES PARA ESO." EDITORA ISABEL DE LOS RÍOS. CARACAS. 1991

126 EKARÉ PUBLISHING HOUSE

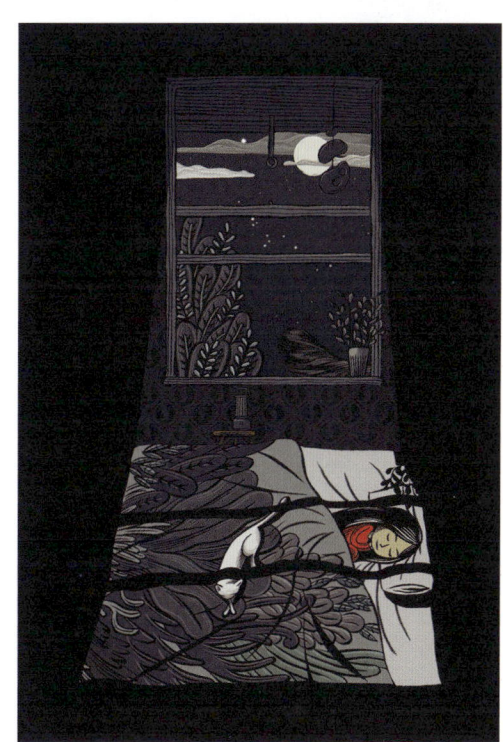

1 WHEN ELISA CAN'T FALL ASLEEP   2 WHEN THE WIND YAWNS   5 TILL NEXT TIME

4 ENCOUNTER WITH ESTEBALDO

3 ELISA IS NOT AFRAID WHEN SHE IS HALF ASLEEP

1   3   4   5

RAMÓN PARÍS
3ERMUNDO.COM

Duermevela (Half asleep) · Indian ink and brush, digital coloring · Fiction

Venezuela · *Caracas, 21 May 1969*

info@3ermundo.com · 0034 662360439

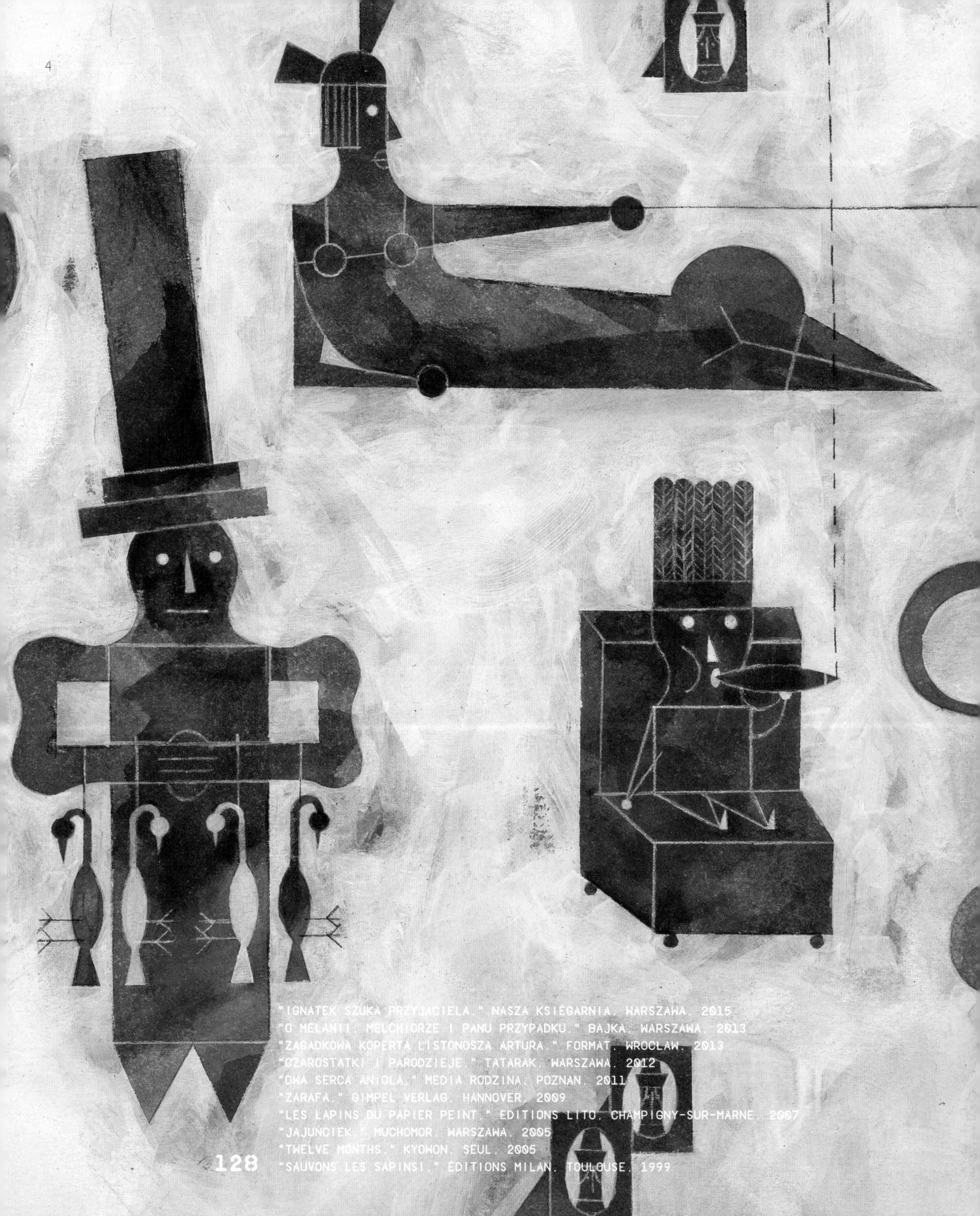

4

1

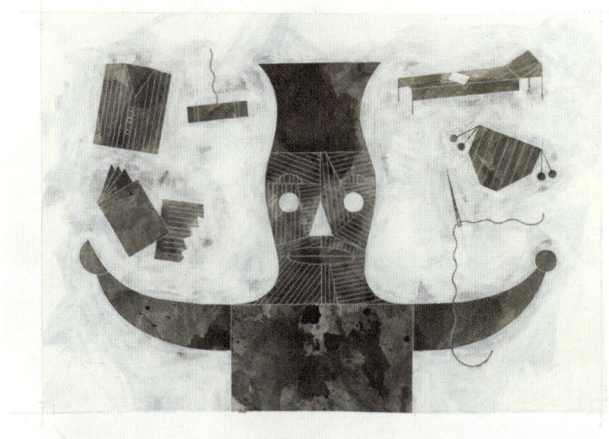

2

3

5

1 ABOUT GYOM. A YOUNG ICE CREAM SELLER FROM THE CITY OF BATUM. WHO WANTED TO BE AN OLD MAN. BECAUSE HE THOUGHT YOUNG PEOPLE HAD NO CHANCE TO GET A GOOD JOB IN LAILONIA   2 ABOUT TAT. WHO TRIED EVERYTHING TO BECOME THE MOST FAMOUS MAN IN THE WORLD   3 ABOUT A WAR THAT BROKE OUT IN THE GORGOLA KINGDOM BETWEEN SUPPORTERS OF DIFFERENT METHODS OF ACHIEVING LONGEVITY   4 ABOUT GIA. PEPI. KAKU. HEJA. HIPA AND KIWI. THE SIBLINGS. WHO HAD SUCH DIFFERENT HABITS THAT THEY WERE ARGUING WITH EACH OTHER ALL THE TIME   5 ABOUT THREE BROTHERS WHO SET OFF ON A JOURNEY IN SEARCH OF WORK. BECAUSE THE BAD AND RICH NEIGHBOR HAD TAKEN THEIR FAMILY LAND. SO THEY HAD NOTHING TO LIVE ON

PAWEL PAWLAK

13 Fairy tales from the Kingdom of Lailonia for Big and Little Folks

Acrylic, black and white pencil • Fiction

Znak Emotikon, Krakow, 2015, ISBN 9788324039005

Poland • *Wroclaw, 16 March 1962*

pepawlak@gazeta.pl • 0048 713988211

4

"LORIS." A BUEN PASO. BARCELONA. TO BE PUBLISHED

"IO DISEGNO." VANVERE EDIZIONI. ROMA. 2015

"JE VEUX ENLEVER LA NUIT." CAMBOURAKIS. PARIS. 2015

"L'UOMO DEI PALLONCINI." TOPIPITTORI. MILANO. 2014

"MISSIONE CASA." FRANCO COSIMO PANINI EDITORE. MODENA. 2013

"EL ACTOR." A BUEN PASO. BARCELONA. 2012

"LA PROMENADE AU MUSÉE." RAMINO. PARIS. 2012

"LA CAVALLA STORNA." RIZZOLI. MILANO. 2012

"FAVOLE DI ESOPO." TOPIPITTORI. MILANO. 2011

"TORNERANNO LE QUATTRO STAGIONI." MONDADORI. MILANO. 2011

"GLI OCCHIALI FANTASTICI." FRANCO COSIMO PANINI EDITORE. MODENA. 2010

"VITA NEL VENTO." FATATRAC. FIRENZE. 2006

3 THE PEOPLE. SURPRISED BY SUCH FURY. TRIED TO FIND SHELTER WHEREVER THEY COULD: CLUTCHING AT THEIR OVERCOATS. SEEKING REFUGE IN SHOPS OR CAFES 4 AN OLD WOMAN. AT THE DOOR OF HER HOME. FELT THE WIND SUDDENLY SNATCH HER ELEGANT HAT WITH THE VEIL THAT HER HUSBAND HAD GIVEN HER YEARS AGO FOR HER BIRTHDAY

3

SIMONE REA
SIMONEREA.COM

Il Vento (The Wind) • Colored pencils, graphite • Fiction
Il Leone Verde Edizioni, Turin, 2016, ISBN 9788865801499

Italy • *Albano Laziale, 27 November 1975*

simonerea@gmail.com • 0039 3493964483

5 "WÄR ICH PIRAT..." PETER HAMMER VERLAG. WUPPERTAL. 2012
"AM LIEBSTEN EINE KATZE." PETER HAMMER VERLAG. WUPPERTAL. 2010
"MIA MIT DEM HUT." PETER HAMMER VERLAG. WUPPERTAL. 2007
"EMIL WIRD SIEBEN." PETER HAMMER VERLAG. WUPPERTAL. 2005

ANDRÉ RÖSLER
DER-ROESLER.DE

Mr. Schmitz Goes to a Concert
Digital media • Fiction
Germany • *Lahr, 7 December 1970*
kontakt@der-roesler.de • 0049 7219212352

5 THE MUSICIANS DISCOVER THE MOUSE

1

LYCÉE CORVISART, PARIS
DIRECTOR: MARIE-LAURE BÉRENGUIER
COORDINATOR: LAURENT CORVAISIER

5

VICKY ROYER
ROYERVICKY.COM

La petite voleuse (The Little Thief) · Mixed media: pencil, posca · Fiction

France · *Bourg-Saint-Maurice, 3 May 1994*

royervicky@gmail.com · 0033 622567726

3

2

4

5

"SUNDAY AT THE MARKET." EKARÉ. BARCELONA. 2016
"TALES OF THE GLOBE 4." PEQUEÑO EDITOR BUENOS AIRES. 2015
"AS TIME WENT BY." COMUNICARTE. BUENOS AIRES / NORD-SÜD. ZÜRICH / KITE.
PIAZZOLA DEL BRENTA (PD) / LA FRAGATINA. FRAGA (HUESCA). 2014-2016
"FOOTPRINTS IN THE SAND." SUDAMERICANA. BUENOS AIRES. 2012
"HUNGRY BUG." ALFAGUARA. BUENOS AIRES. 2012
"THE LITTLE MATCH GIRL." MINEDITION. BARGTEHEIDE. 2011
"THE BEST TALES FROM THE ARABIAN NIGHTS." CLARÍN. BUENOS AIRES. 2008
"THE BEST TALES OF GOBLINS." CLARÍN. BUENOS AIRES. 2008
"MISSION DENT DE LAIT." BAYARD PRESSE. MONTROUGE. 2007
"THE CROWS OF PEARBLOSSOM." SM. ARGENTINA. BUENOS AIRES 2007
"RAPUNZEL." SOL 90. BARCELONA. 2006
"THE SHOEMAKER AND THE ELVES." SOL 90. BARCELONA. 2006
"THE LITTLE MATCH-SELLER." SOL 90. BARCELONA. 2006
"ALICE IN WONDERLAND." SOL 90. BARCELONA. 2006

JOSÉ SANABRIA

JOSESANABRIAILUSTRACION.BLOGSPOT.COM

Una hoja en el viento (A sheet in the wind)

Acrylic • Fiction

Colombia • *Bogotá, 17 February 1969*

josesanabriaacevedo@gmail.com • **0054 1149367729**

ANNA SARVIRA

BEHANCE.NET/ANNASARVIR096B

"No adults!"

Children's Poetry

Digital media • Fiction

Ukraine • *Zaporizhzhya, 6 September 1986*

anna.sarvira@gmail.com • 00380 955008489

"HEDGEHOG VILGELM." VIVAT. KHARKIV. 2016
"A COIN." BRATSKE. KIEV. 2015
"LITTLE RED RIDING HOOD." MOZAIKA SINTEZ. MOSCOW. 2015
"PUSS IN BOOTS." MOZAIKA SINTEZ. MOSCOW. 2015
"MCBROOM'S WONDERFUL FARM." GRANI-T. KIEV. 2012
"MYSHA'S MOUSES." GRANI-T. KIEV. 2011
"DARYNA AND THE HUB OF THE UNIVERSE." GRANI-T. KIEV. 2007
"NAUGHTY GRANNY." GRANI-T. KIEV. 2006

1

1

2

3

4

5 HE FINDS HIS HANDS EXPLORING THE RIVER STONES

4 LEAVE THE CITY BEHIND

3 THE SEARCH BEGINS

2 A HOME-SHAPED PRISON

LAURA SAVINA
LAUSVANK.TUMBLR.COM

The Man Who Lost Himself · Graphite, stencils, digital collage, gouache · Fiction

Italy · *Frascati, 29 October 1987*

laurasavina.mela@gmail.com · 0039 3389092709

1

5

CRISTÓBAL SCHMAL

ARTNOMONO.COM

Atacama • Watercolor, ink, pigments, collage • Fiction

Chile • *Arica, 10 November 1977*

info@artnomono.com • **0049 1635883933**

"EL BOSQUE DENTRO DE MÍ." FONDO DE CULTURA ECONÓMICA. CIUDAD DE MÉXICO. 2016
"UN DISFRAZ EQUIVOCADO." NÓRDICA EDITORIAL. MADRID. 2015
"LA PIEL EXTENSA." EDELVIVES. MADRID. 2013
"CAPERUCITA ROJA." NARVAL EDITORES. MADRID. 2011

ADOLFO SERRA
ADOLFOSERRA.BLOGSPOT.COM.ES

Dr. Rampa Rattanrithikul's Museum of World Insects and Natural Wonders

Collage, engraving, pencils, wax, watercolors • Non fiction

Spain • *Teruel, 31 August 1980*

serra.adolfo@gmail.com • 0034 606979857

"JOM JOMAK." NAZAR ART PUBLICATION. TEHRAN. 2010
"KAFSH HAYE AHANI." SHABAVIZ PUBLISHING COMPANY. TEHRAN. 2009
"DEL BE DARYA." SHABAVIZ PUBLISHING COMPANY. TEHRAN. 2007
"PEYVAND." SHABAVIZ PUBLISHING COMPANY. TEHRAN. 2006
"POUPÉE DE SUCRE." LIRABELLE. NÎMES. 2006
"ZARBAL." SHABAVIZ PUBLISHING COMPANY. TEHRAN. 2005
"HELI FESSGHELI." PEYDAYESH PUBLISHING COMPANY. TEHRAN. 2002
"PIRE CHANGI." SHABAVIZ PUBLISHING COMPANY. TEHRAN. 2002
"QEYR AZ KHODA HICHKAS NABOOD." SHABAVIZ PUBLISHING COMPANY. TEHRAN. 2001
"FARSHID." SHABAVIZ PUBLISHING COMPANY. TEHRAN. 2001
"SHAHRZAD. SHABAVIZ PUBLISHING COMPANY. TEHRAN. 2000
"QESE HAYE MAN." SHABAVIZ PUBLISHING COMPANY. TEHRAN. 2000
"DISHAB MAHTAB AROOSI KARD." SOROOSH PUBLICATION. TEHRAN. 2000

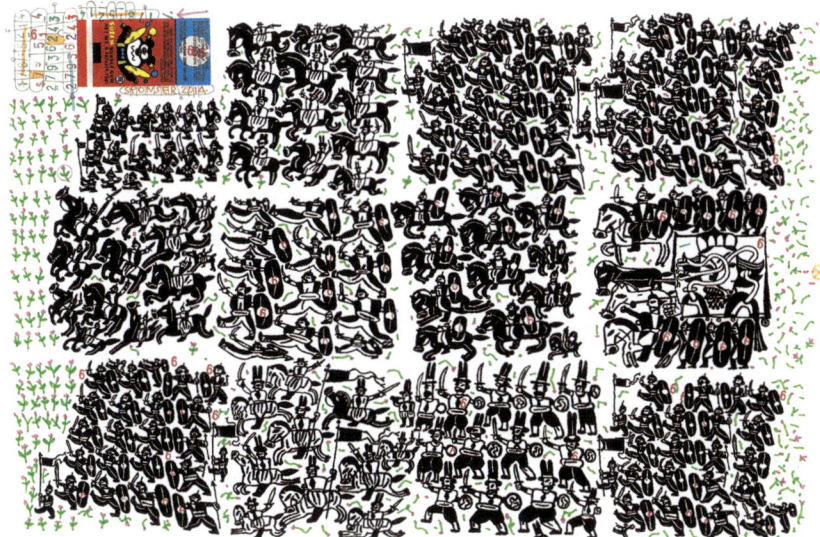

2015

2015

2014

2

3

4

FARSHID SHAFIEY

FARSHIDSHAFI.COM

Zahak • Mixed media • Fiction
Nazar Publications, Tehran, to be published
Iran • *Tehran, 6 March 1969*
farshid47@gmail.com • 001 9179002451

148

TINA SIUDA

TINASIUDA.COM

Pebble and the Beast • Gouache, graphite • Fiction

Poland • *Szczecin, 12 June 1987*

tinasiudababa@gmail.com • 00351 918851365

1 MARSHMALLOW NIGHT
2 TRICKY BEAST
3 ONE CAN NEVER HAVE TOO MANY FINGERS
4 SOMETIMES EVEN ROCKS CRY
5 PEBBLE'S FAMILY REUNIONS ARE ALWAYS FUN

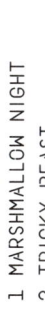

4

3

5

1

Smeda Rmeda — A Moroccan Tale · Digital media · Fiction

Israel · *Jerusalem, 9 May 1987*

kinoanoa@gmail.com · 0049 15787712152

NOA SNIR

NOASNIR.COM

1   2   4

"CERDO CERDO." A BUEN PASO. BARCELONA. TO BE PUBLISHED
"LILLI: DELFINI ALLA DERIVA." LA NUOVA FRONTIERA JUNIOR. ROMA. 2016
"LILLI: LE TIGRI NON BACIANO I LEONI." LA NUOVA FRONTIERA JUNIOR. ROMA. 2015
"THE TEMPEST." TEEN ELI READERS. LORETO. 2015
"LILLI: VIETATO PARLARE AGLI ELEFANTI." LA NUOVA FRONTIERA JUNIOR. ROMA. 2014
"I PROMESSI SPOSI." LETTURE GRADUATE ELI. RECANATI. 2014

5

CRISTINA SPANÒ
CRISTINASPANO.COM

Dove Porta Questa Porta? (Where Does This Door Lead?)

Digital media • Fiction

Italy • *Rome, 2 December 1985*

cristinaspano@gmail.com • 0034 673741026

"AU MARCHÉ JE CHOISIS..." HELIUM. PARIS. 2017
"IL SEGRETO DELLE COSE." TOPIPITTORI. MILANO. 2017
"FAVOLOSO NATALE." EMME EDIZIONI. TRIESTE. 2016
"MATEMATICA AMICA." FELTRINELLI. MILANO. 2016
"IN OGNI PINOCCHIO." TOPIPITTORI. MILANO. 2016
"TOUTES LES CHOSES AVEC LESQUELLES..." HELIUM. PARIS. 2015
"NON PIANGERE CIPOLLA." MONDADORI. MILANO. 2015
"CHE NOTTE É QUESTA!." EDIZIONI EL. TRIESTE. 2014
"ET TOI, OÙ HABITES-TU?." JOIE DE LIRE. GENÉVE. 2014
"MATEMAGO." FELTRINELLI. MILANO. 2014
"CHEZ NOUS." EDITIONS AMATERRA. LYON. 2014
"VITA DA CANI." FELTRINELLI. MILANO. 2013
"QUANTE FACCE." EMME EDIZIONI. TRIESTE. 2013
"COSA CI STA IN VENTUNO PER VENTOTTO CENTIMETRI (21X28 CM)?."
LA MARGHERITA EDIZIONI. MILANO. 2013
"FIABE DI ANIMALI MAGICI." MONDADORI. MILANO. 2013
"TI TENGO." SAVE THE CHILDREN-DRAFTFCB. 2011

GAIA STELLA

GAIASTELLA.COM

In & Out

Stamps and digital media • Non Fiction

Italy • *Milan, 9 July 1982*

info@gaiastella.com • **0039 3498427654**

1

2

3

4

1 WE MEET UNEXPECTEDLY IN AN OLD ABANDONED BOTTLE CAP FACTORY 2 TOGETHER WE START A NEW JOURNEY. WANDERING THROUGH THE CITY 3 SURPRISES AND AMAZING EVENTS HAPPEN DURING THE ADVENTURE 4 NO MATTER WHAT HAPPENS, WE HAVE EACH OTHER

YU TENG
BEHANCE.NET/TENGYU

Way Back Home • Digital media • Fiction
Locus Publishing Company, Taipei, 2016, ISBN 9789862137154

Taiwan • *Taipei, 8 October 1985*

hahatengteng@gmail.com • 00886 963322086

2

"ÇA CHANGE TOUT!." L'ATELIER DU POISSON SOLUBLE. PUY-EN-VELAY. TO BE PUBLISHED
"À QUOI RÊVE MARCO." ÉDITIONS DU ROUERGUE. ARLES. TO BE PUBLISHED
"LA TULIPE NOIRE." LECTURES ELI. RECANATI. 2016
"MANON LESCAUT." LECTURES ELI. RECANATI. 2014
"NOIR GRAND." ÉDITIONS DU ROUERGUE. ARLES. 2012/SANHA PUBLISHING CO. SEOUL. 2014
"FAVOLE PER BAMBINI RUBACUORI." EDITORI INTERNAZIONALI RIUNITI. ROMA. 2013
"BODAS DE SANGRE." LECTURAS ELI. RECANATI. 2013
"A MIDSUMMER NIGHT'S DREAM." ELI READERS. RECANATI. 2013
"CONFESSO CHE HO DESIDERATO." KITE EDIZIONI/PASSEPARTOUT. PIAZZOLA SUL BRENTA (PD). 2011

DANIELA TIENI

DANITIENI.TUMBLR.COM

Connessioni (Connections) • Digital media • Fiction

Italy • *Rome, 10 January 1982*

dani.tieni@gmail.com • 0039 3402989261

1

2

UNIVERSITY OF FINE ARTS OF POZNAŃ
DIRECTOR: WOJCIECH HORA
COORDINATOR: MIROSLAV ADAMCZYK

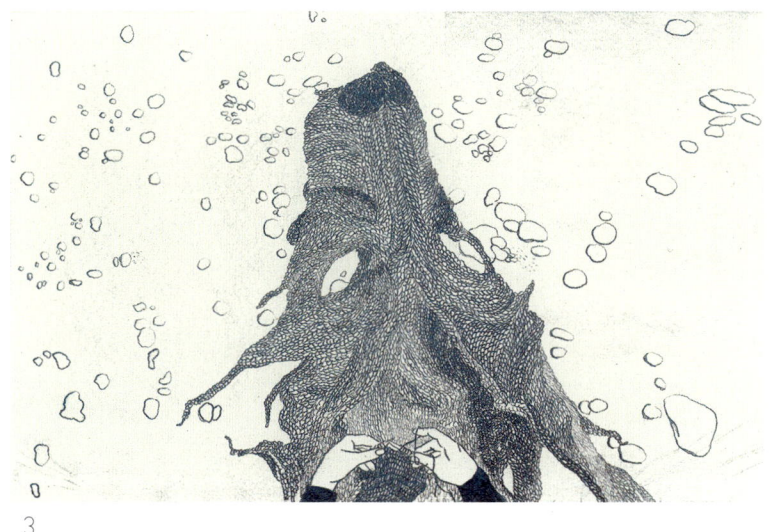

3

4

MARTA TOMIAK
BEHANCE.NET/KTOPITAS

The Meeting · Monotype · Fiction

Poland · *Wolsztyn, 1 February 1990*

ktopitas@gmail.com · 0048 691861897

1

"ROBINSON CRUSOE." HELBLING READERS. 2016
"IN MEZZO ALLA FIABA." TOPIPITTORI. MILANO. 2015
"DESDE LOS OJOS DE LUCAS." A BUEN PASO. BARCELONA. 2015
"THE RIGHT THING." HELBLING READERS. 2015
"MOBY DICK." ELI READERS. RECANATI. 2015
"HOKA HEY." PRATIBIANCHI EDIZIONI. MILANO. 2013
"GANDHI — UN PUGNO DI SALE." PRATIBIANCHI EDIZIONI. MILANO. 2013
"GORDON PYM." ELI EDIZIONI. RECANATI. 2013
"L'ULTIMO SEGRETO." NOI ASSOCIAZIONE EDIZIONI. VERONA. 2012
"UN PAESE BAMBINO." GIANNINO STOPPANI EDIZIONI. BOLOGNA. 2011
"PEL DI CAROTA." ELI EDIZIONI. RECANATI. 2011
"IL MALATO IMMAGINARIO." ELI EDIZIONI. RECANATI
"LA METAMORFOSI." ELI EDIZIONI. RECANATI
"L'EDUCAZIONE SENTIMENTALE." ELI EDIZIONI. RECANATI

2

5

ARIANNA VAIRO

ARIANNAVAIRO.COM

Pollicino (Tom Thumb) • Brushes and ink, digital coloring • Fiction

Italy • *Milan, 25 December 1985*

arianvairo@gmail.com • 0039 3342944172

"EDITH & EGON SCHIELE." LEOPOLD. AMSTERDAM. 2014
"LETTERDROMEN MET DO." QUERIDO. AMSTERDAM. 2007
"BOKJE." QUERIDO. AMSTERDAM. 2001
"HET BERGJE SPEK." QUERIDO. AMSTERDAM. 1989
"DE AVONTUREN VAN LENA LENA." QUERIDO. AMSTERDAM. 1986
"HENKELMAN. ONS HENKELMANNETJE." QUERIDO. AMSTERDAM. 1986

Lettersoep (Alphabet Soup)

Watercolor, colored pencil, digital media • Fiction

Querido Kinderboeken Uitgeverij, Amsterdam, 2015, ISBN 9789045118710

HARRIËT VAN REEK

HARRIETVANREEK.NL

The Netherlands • *Leiden, 21 November 1957*

harrietvanreek@dds.nl • 0031 624224377

4

3

5

VENDI VERNIĆ

CARGOCOLLECTIVE.COM/VENDIVV   BEHANCE.NET/VENDI_VV

The Overcoat (short story by N.V. Gogol) • Colored pencils, watercolors, tempera, acrylic colors, ink, ballpoint pen, collage • Fiction

Croatia • *Zagreb, 2 October 1991*

vendi.vv@gmail.com • 00385 915324482

3

"STILL OPTIMISTIC - ARTISTS PAINT DUDU GEVA." KINNERET ZMORA BITAN DVIR
PUBLISHING HOUSE. MODIIN. 2015
"BANANA MOON PARTY." MODAN PUBLISHING HOUSE. TEL AVIV. 2012
"GOOD NIGHT MONSTER." AM OVED PUBLISHERS. TEL AVIV. 2012
"THE SCATTERED MAN OF AZAR'S VILLAGE." AM OVED PUBLISHERS. TEL AVIV. 2011

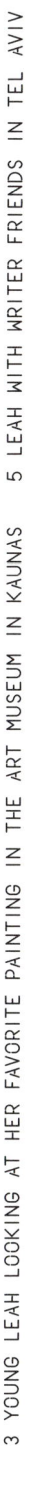

5

NATALIE WAKSMAN SHENKER

NATALIEWAKSMAN.CARBONMADE.COM

My Aunt Leah Goldberg by No-one • Pencils, watercolor, digital collage • Fiction
Kinneret Zmora-Bitan Dvir Publishing House, Modi In, 2016, ISBN 9789655661729

Israel • *Eilat, 15 October 1979*

natilw@yahoo.com • 00972 46387289

"THE FUR TRAP." FANCY BUTCHER PRESS/CATAPULTE RECORDS. LONDON. 2014

4

KEVIN WARD

INKOPINKO.COM

The Hoarse Heckler • Ink, watercolor, digital media • Fiction

Ireland/Canada • *Ottawa, 3 August 1975*

kevin@inkopinko.com • 0044 7479662643

1 A BOY AND A GIRL ARE CHASING A FLYING FISH IN THE TOWN   2 THEY KEEP CHASING THE FLYING FISH THROUGH THE SAVANNAH AND DESERT   3 THE FLYING FISH FLIES AWAY THROUGH A QUIRKY JUNGLE   4 THE CHILDREN KEEP CHASING THE FLYING FISH OVER THE VAST OCEAN HOPPING FROM ISLAND TO ISLAND

"MAAAPS!." STUDIO SSS. HUDSON COHIOD. 2013

AUNYARAT WATANABE

AW-ILLUSTRATIONS.COM

Chasing Flying Fish • Gouache, pencil, pen, collage • Fiction

Japan • *Hyogo, 25 January 1975*

watanabe@aw-illustrations.com • **0081 0366764719**

1

FIERE

2

5

"DIE MAGISCHE FLASCHENPOST - PIKKOFINTES ZWEITE REISE." KJM-VERLAG.
HAMBURG. 2016
"DIE SIEBEN MAGISCHEN KLABAUTERKNOTEN - PIKKOFINTES ERSTE REISE."
KJM-VERLAG. HAMBURG. 2014

HAW HAMBURG
DIRECTOR: CLAUS-DIETER WACKER

3

LENA WINKEL

WINKEL-ILLUSTRATION.DE

Untitled • Watercolor • Fiction

Germany • *Kirchen (Sieg), 22 December 1993*

lena_winkel@gmx.de • 0049 151237413205

2

3

JUI-CHE WU
WUJUICHE.COM

The Shepherd Said Goodbye • Collage, watercolor, pencil, carbon pencil, colored pencil, ink • Fiction

Taiwan • *Taoyuan County, 4 December 1992*

wujuiche.tw@gmail.com • 00886 988793291

4

"VITOR E O INVISÍVEL " SESI-SP EDITORA. SÃO PAULO. 2013

ACCADEMIA DI BELLE ARTI DI BOLOGNA
DIRECTOR: ENRICO FORNAROLI
COORDINATOR: LUIGI RAFFAELLI

3 WHEN HE WANTS TO SEE THE HORIZON IN THE DISTANCE. THE BOY WALKS INTO THE WOODS. HE GOES INTO THE FOREST AND SEARCHES FOR HIS LIANA
4 THE BOY'S LIANA FORMS THE PATH FOR ANTS. FORMS A BRIDGE BETWEEN TREES AND NESTS AND LAIRS AND BRANCHES. AT TIMES SHE ACTS AS A
TELEPHONE. SHE TELLS STORIES TO THE SICK BABY ANIMALS THAT MUSTN'T LEAVE THEIR NESTS. AND CONNECTS THE TREETOPS

BRUNA XIMENES

XIMENESBRUNA.TUMBLR.COM

O Menino e o Cipo (The Boy and the Liana)

Markers, pencils and digital media • Fiction

Editora Espiral, Recife, to be published

Brazil • *São Paulo, 9 March 1993*

bruna.tximenes@gmail.com • 0039 3884237390

1

3

"AIUEON." PARADE BOOKS. OSAKA. 2014
"MERRY-GO-ROUND NO CHISANA UMA TAI NI." GENTOSHA. TOKYO. 2012

4

5

MAMORU YAMAMOTO

MAMORUYAMAMOTO.COM

Little Pero's Magic Tongue • Digital media, collage, colored pencils • Fiction

Japan • *Tokyo, 11 October 1960*

mamoroll@purple.plala.or.jp • 0081 459349633

3

"THE STEADFAST TIN SOLDIER." ENCHANTED LION BOOKS. BROOKLYN. 2016
"BEASTLY VERSE." ENCHANTED LION BOOKS. BROOKLYN. 2015

"RE TIGRE." ORECCHIO ACERBO. ROMA. 2014

5

4

1

JOOHEE YOON

JOOHEEYOON.COM

Insects · Screen printing · Non fiction

USA · *Seoul, 21 February 1989*

jooheeyoon@gmail.com · 001 9788283427

TURNING THE PAGE MAKES IT POSSIBLE TO CONSTRUCT THINGS, TO TRIGGER SURPRISES MOVING TO THE NEXT PAGE

The world-famous artist and graphic designer KATSUMI KOMAGATA was born in 1953 in Japan. After having worked in the world of fashion and graphic design, Komagata's interest in the field of children's books was aroused after the birth of his daughter at the beginning of the 1990s, and he has since received many international honors. Today Komagata shows his works and conducts encounters and workshops for adults and children all over the world. He lives in Tokyo.

What things in your background as a graphic designer made you a better picture book author?

I constantly try to solve problems in communication. Therefore, face the facts, find problems behind them, and derive ways to solve them. For example, when my daughter was three months old, I had no idea how I could communicate with her and could not even tell her who I was, but I created cards that I could share with her, and as a result we gradually became able to know each other, and eventually we were able to share the communication. These ideas are largely due to so-called visual contacts that I have tried as a graphic designer.

In which ways can the book, as an object, enhance the expressive power of illustration?

Illustration will be flat when it is printed as a book, but there are pages in the book. Turning the page makes it possible to construct things, to trigger surprises moving to the next page, stimulating the reader's interest. Technically there are die cutting, folding, pop-up techniques, etc. In addition, the texture of the papers also stimulates the sense of touch as well as the sense of sight.

In your view, what should be the ultimate aim of a picture book?

In the market, picture books are created for children. It's true though, if the book is raised to the level of art, it can become a prized possession. The experience and time that we share with the book can become a great and cherished memory.

Who has been your greatest influence as a picture book author? What is the most important lesson an illustrator can learn from his or her work?

Bruno Munari, Leo Lionni, Iela Mari, Saul Bass, Paul Rand and many others. They can teach you to face reality, to derive a solution for sharing.

What role has illustration for children played in the formation of your visual culture?

The question can only have an obvious answer.

For all the kids of my generation, more or less, it was normal to spend entire days looking at picture books. Thanks to long quiet days imposed by minor maladies followed by not unwelcome periods of convalescence, without television. Damsels, knights, warriors, animals with humanized features, mythological rituals, even Dante-esque complexities filled the time. So we gobbled up—together with our first spoonfuls of something like Nutella—a sense of adventure, i.e. the sense of life, from the gorgeous illustrations of those beautiful books that are still "alive" today in some hidden cranny of our homes.

I had the good luck to have a bibliophile father, who taught me that passion. And I remember, first of all, the extraordinary and very institutional series of the "Scala d'Oro" (published by UTET) that offered summaries of the classics of not just Western, not just Catholic literature, in a universal overview with volumes bound in greenish gray, and lots of space for illustrations, right from the cover.

Much of my visual culture came from these books. Gustavino, a very elegant illustrator, fascinated me for his erudite ability to sum up fantastic worlds in very detailed plates, flashes of beauty that infinitely enhanced the adventures, the narrated episodes, the images that formed in my head and pulsated in nocturnal memory. Still in the "Scala d'Oro" series, there were amazing illustrations by other giants, the makers of these

FONTS, DESIGNED TYPOGRAPHICAL CHARACTERS, SPATIAL RIGOR OR EXTREME FREEDOM ARE THE ELEMENTS THAT GIVE VISUAL POWER TO ILLUSTRATION

ITALO LUPI is one of the leading figures of Italian graphic design. He has worked on exhibit design, coordinated graphic design projects and publications. He has been an image consultant for La Rinascente, IBM Italia and Triennale di Milano, then art director of "Domus" and, from 1992 to 2007, managing editor and art director of "Abitare." He has received many international honors, including two Compassi d'Oro awards and the Bronze Medal of the International Design Awards of Los Angeles in 2012.

books: from Nicouline (very geometric and architectural) to Carlo Bisi, to Piero Bernardini. . . .

I loved them, but I considered this praiseworthy series a bit too rigid in its continuously repetitive layouts. So it was nice to seek refuge in the magical worlds of the English illustrators, published in precious volumes, where the wonderfully printed images were protected by white tracing paper. I remember the sounds and odors of these books, where the illustrations of Arthur Rackham or another post-Victorian like Edmund Dulac, in their absolute masterpieces *Gulliver's Travels* and the *Niebelungen*, mixed fairies, gnomes, Gargantua and the English forests, stormy skies and dapper London bobbies.

An early passion, an anglophilia I would rediscover, shortly thereafter, with realistic illustrators who in those years were already helping us to understand a Fabian, utterly British socialism, expressed precisely in the authenticity of the graphic sign, describing the normality of the life of the populace. Unforgettable afternoons after the eagerly awaited arrival of "Corriere dei Piccoli," which often replaced the "speech bubbles" of comic strips with little poemlets of storytelling that helped us to appreciate the inimitable drawings of the sophisticated Sto (Sergio Tofano), the Nouveau masterpieces of Antonio Rubino, the brightly colored geometric inventions of the peerless Angoletta; inventions that suggest today the name of another magician, Alessandro Mendini.

And then there were the marvelous comics. Starting with the true Mickey Mouse of the time, of Walt Disney, of course, but where the grease pencil of Floyd Gottfredson managed to convey an America of the Roosevelt era perfectly in tune with the image shown to us of a certain Hollywood by Frank Capra.

And then Milton Caniff, Battaglia, Albertarelli, Hugo Pratt, Mario Faustinelli, Bellavitis, Al Capp, Alex Raymond. . . . Powerful narrators of unforgettable adventures. All this played a fundamental role in my visual education.

Dialogue with illustration is a constant in your work as a graphic artist. What does illustration add to a book or a magazine?

What does illustration add to a story, a newspaper, a magazine? It grants what photography grants, but with a capacity for synthesis and summary you can guide and render expressive and functional, with a bit more sharpness and the freedom to use illustrations, drawings, in different ways: breaking them into segments, enlarging certain portions, shrinking them and multiplying them. You have to have a good relationship with the artist who draws, and so you can afford the luxury, the freedom of making the illustration the prima donna of an entire magazine issue or book.

I have been the art director, first, and then for long, wonderful years the editor of architecture magazines. There it was easy for me, though not so predictable in that context, to make extensive use of illustrations on covers and for articles, as the true colorful pillars of the whole publication.

My companions were (among many others) Bau Scarabottolo, Andrea Ventura (then still unknown), Guidotti and (above all) Steven Guarnaccia, as well as Joost Swarte, David Gentleman, George Hardie, Jeff Fisher.

Does a somehow conflictual dialectic exist in the relationship between graphic designer and illustrator?
Of course a dialectic exists, and the mutual exchange of ideas, but it is never conflictual. We choose each other for affinities.

When talking about illustrated books, what part of the visual power of an image is intrinsic to the illustration itself and what part depends on the way it is placed on the page, the way it establishes a dialogue with the text and the book-object?
Alphabets, fonts, designed typographical characters, spatial rigor or extreme freedom are the elements that give visual power to illustration in a coordination of aims that is the true wealth of a book.

In the harmony of a page, an illustration made smaller or larger, central or lateral, in color or tonal in a game of whites, blacks, grays, functions in a complex way, of course, but it balances full and empty zones, i.e. it does its job of illustration. Which can be done by a photograph or even by an enlarged initial letter, a flourish that is functional for the story. Typography, drawing, photography: my lifelong friends, indispensable tools of the trade. Traveling companions on different trains.

First published in the United States of America in 2017 by Chronicle Books LLC.

Originally published in Italy in 2017 by Maurizio Corraini s.r.l.

ILLUSTRATORS ANNUAL 2017

Book design
PIETRO CORRAINI
& CORRAINISTUDIO

Translations
EUGENIA DURANTE
TRANSITING.EU/S.PICCOLO

Image processing
MAISTRI FOTOLITO, VERONA

ISBN 978-1-4521-6347-5

Library of Congress Cataloging-in-Publication Data available.

Manufactured in China.

Interior design by Pietro Corraini & corrainiStudio.
Cover design by Ryan Hayes.
Typeset in ARGN & Rooney.

10 9 8 7 6 5 4 3 2 1

CHRONICLE BOOKS LLC
680 SECOND STREET
SAN FRANCISCO, CALIFORNIA 94107

CHRONICLE BOOKS—we see things differently. Become part of our community at www.chroniclebooks.com.